WOMEN WRITE THE WAR

WOMEN WRITE THE WAR

The Voices of Women Behind Operation Iraqi Freedom

Bee Pedersen

St. John's Press
Tuscaloosa, AL

Each story in this anthology represents the author's experiences and opinions and is not necessarily the opinion of all the writers represented. The featured quotations are not related to any specific story and are not necessarily the opinion of all the writers. They are the results of interviews and research, and are meant to share emotional pictures.

A portion of the proceeds from this anthology will be donated to charity. The specific organizations will be chosen on a year-by-year basis. Proceeds will go to organizations supporting children who have been affected by war or terrorism.

••••••••••••••••••••••••••••••••••

ISBN 0-9710551-7-3

Printed in the United States of America

Published by St. John's Press, Tuscaloosa, AL

IT consulting by Lyle Osborne, Angus Consulting, Inc.

Stories collected, collated and edited by Bee Pedersen

Book cover design by Leopard

Book cover photo by U.S. Army Staff Sergeant Marvin L. Daniels
Specialist Janet Sutter provides security in Baghdad, Iraq

Book cover photo by U.S. Air Force Senior Airman Jason Neal
Staff Sergeant Chris Walton hugs his wife, Jennifer, on the flight line, May 10, 2003, after returning home from Operation Iraqi Freedom

Book cover, Iraqi map, courtesy of the University of Texas Library

Women Write the War: The Voices of Women Behind Operation Iraqi Freedom

Women's studies/sociology of peace and war/history/Iraq/Pedersen—1958

First Edition, July 2004

Visit Bee Pedersen at **www.womenwritethewar.net**

Dedication

To our brave soldiers and their families.
And
To those fighting without uniforms,
Next to our soldiers.

For you, Kevin, in Iraq.
For Dad and your brothers at home.
I love you!

Mom

Contents

Foreword

Women Write the War **is one of those books that seems as if** it has always been with us. It is the voice of the military woman, the woman who loves and waits at home alone with her unspeakable fears for her beloved warrior. The authors give voice to a slice of the American experience as authentic as the Pacific and Atlantic coasts, and all the beautiful landscape that joins them. The cry from the heart of love is here, a very American and fine clean love that chooses to support and wait and not to forget.

When a soldier, marine, sailor, airman or coast guardsman goes to war, he or she takes a whole family with him or her. While the one at war knows fear and loss directly, those of us left behind know it only second hand. We are left with nightmares rather than facts. The women writers herein have opened their innermost hearts to view, so that their loved ones not be forgotten or go un-thanked, and so that others may know those who waited and watched.

As a "military dad" whose marine son served for 11 months in the Middle East in 2003 and 2004, I identified with this book, but more importantly, with the strong women who wrote it. They speak for all military parents. They speak for me. Thank you!

Frank Schaeffer
May 27,2004

Frank is a writer and the author of *Faith Of Our Sons—A Father's Wartime Diary*, Avalon, NY 2004

Voices from the Heart

For most people, April 4, 2003 was nothing special—just a day like any other day. For my family, though, and thousands of other military family members, it was a day that would change our lives forever. At midnight, I answered a phone call from our son telling me that he was about to board the plane leaving for Iraq to support Operation Iraqi Freedom. That was the moment I realized that the voices from my heart were going to dominate my life for an unknown period of time. In that moment, *Women Write the War* was born.

As I began to recover from my own self-pity, I became aware that my story connected to the stories of others, forming a united voice of women. I put out the word inviting other women to share their stories, and before I knew it, a unique band of sisters had been established between women of all ages from all over the world.

The challenges of war are mostly pictured through the eyes of men—young, brave men—because young men have been, and still are, the majority of the soldiers sent to war. With *Women Write the War*, I wish to portray the brave women fighting for survival, whether on the battlefield or at home.

Creating such a portrait is hard to do. For many of the women involved in this book, honesty has been difficult to face and share. Sharing your deepest feelings in public, during probably the most traumatic time in your life, is a brave thing to do and should be treated with the utmost respect.

In gathering those stories, I have been very fortunate to meet and make friends with so many wonderful people, all of whom, in some way, have been affected by Operation Iraqi Freedom. Although a traumatic time for my family and me, this journey has brought forth many life-changing and positive experiences.

I am honored to embark on this journey with you.

Bee Pedersen

April 2004

Acknowledgments

I feel so rich having so many compassionate, encouraging and talented people around me. Fearing that in this very moment, I will forget someone—someone very important for this book. My family and I still wish to make an important effort thanking you all. Thank you to everyone who supported and helped me with this project. I am very grateful and honored to be able to share the final result with the world; this significant anthology. Without you this wouldn't have been possible.

A special thank you to the amazing women contributing to this book. Without you, your family and your brave soldiers, this book would never have been possible. You will always be in my heart!

My oldest son Kevin; thank you for everything you do to make this world a better place. I love you so much and I'm so proud of you! My wonderful husband, Leif, and our two wonderful sons, Christoffer and David—thank you for your loving support and for always being my sunshine, especially during a very dark time for us all. I'm so proud of you and I love you so much!

My brilliant publisher Chuck Boyle, St. John's Press, it has been such a great experience working with you. Your passion and involvement in this book's final stage has just been awesome. You know what it means to be a soldier and how important it is to tell these stories for the future. Thank you!

The talented, creative team at Leopard for designing the powerful book cover—thank you, I love the cover. What a great team you are!

A huge thank you to Bob Babcock, President, Americans Remembered, Inc., for your daily updates about our troops in Iraq. What a remarkable effort you have made in supporting our military families and friends. You provided a 'secret' window into our soldiers' life in Iraq, for those of us 'left behind'.

My wonderful and loving family in Denmark, especially my mother, brother and sister and their families—so far away and yet so close—thank you all for giving me such a strong foundation and for always supporting me in my projects. To my dear Mother-in-law, thank you for your strong support and interest in my project. I love you all!

And to you Dad, I know you're cheering from the other side. What a great role model you are. I love you and miss you so much!

My dear friend Author Patti Parr, thank you for your advice, ideas and for encouraging me to move on.

The University of Texas Library for allowing me to use the map of Iraq for the front cover. Thank you for reaching out!

Thank you, Raelynne J. Bayne, A1C, USAF, Kathleen Matthews, TSgt, USAF, Chief, Information Management SAF/PANM, Anna Siegel, ILT, USAF Air Combat Command Public Affairs, and Amber Millerchip, 2LT, USAF AETC/PAN for supporting my project and helping me spread the word.

My very dear friends, Faith and Rod Roberts, for checking documents and for keeping me up and running—thank you for that!

Writer Georgia Richardson—a.k.a. Queen Jawjaw—for your 'first eye' recommendations on the manuscript. Thank you for being such a positive person. My dear "Austin WriterGrrls" for support and comforting words. Thank you to Debra and Ruth Winegarten for your strong belief in this book. All my very dear friends, close and far away, thank you for listening to my worries and for supporting me in yet another project. Listing your names would make a book of its own. I love you all!

To everyone supporting Kevin and his comrades—wherever they serve—with letters, care-packages, prayers, healing light, or in other ways: thank you for being such caring persons.

Journalist Jim Swift, KXAN, for supporting this book initiative and helping me in getting the word out. You too, know for sure, what it means having a son in harms way. Thanks for reaching out my friend!

Represented news channels; thank you for allowing me to present these poignant stories in an important news and time perspective.

Reporter Christiana Amanpour, CNN, thank you for your comforting and supporting words. Radio host, Lonny Stern, thank you for your interest and support. Attorney and friend John Fortkort, and attorney Randy Houston, thank you for reaching out. And, thank you, Attorney Susan J. Arenella and Attorney Paul Skeith, for your legal advice.

The unknown woman, man and child who just happened to cross my road—thank you for your consoling and encouraging words.

And to everyone who makes an effort to make this world a better place for all of us!

Thank you!

Yellow Ribbon, Fort Hood, Texas
March 2004

"War brings sorrow, despair and casualties on both sides. A grieving heart does not have a nationality."

Women Write the War

WE open our hearts
So please step closer

It's okay you don't know what to say
You see WE don't know what to feel

WE wanna share it with you
Even you cannot carry our burden

WE wanna paint the picture
Even you cannot put it on your wall

WE wanna replay the sounds
Even you cannot hear it all

WE wanna hold a moment of your attention
in exchange for weeks, months and years
and maybe
just maybe
you will wonder and understand.

Poem One

By Kim Lane

Penned the first day the bombing began in Iraq, 2003.

This day finds eyes sharing time between the monitor
and the TV,
two of many distractions from this erupting Spring.
Outside, the prattle and chirp
of delirious children
oblivious to the morphing world
captivated by the emerging leaves and chill
wafts through the window
and harmonizes with the
global hum
of churning grief, pain and concern
that floats like a thick new atmospheric layer
just above the Texas clouds.

Poem Two

By Kim Lane

This one was written mid-war, after a particularly deadly week.

"In the dark time will there also be singing?"
"Yes, there will be singing about the dark time."
—Bertolt Brecht

This week finds us gathering our breath
like focused gardeners of the green.
Closing eyes to the insistent sun,
resisting the lure of clouds,
turning from buds,
in order to share an uninterrupted moment
of the darkness
with the other side,
and sing.

Kim Lane is a writer in Austin, TX, and the editor of www.austinmama.com.

Mothers and Grandmothers

Bee Pedersen

Renate "Rain" Nietzold

Charlene Sawyer Family

Margee Willy, grandson Dustin, and grandfather Loren E. Patterson

Janet Witt

Sheree Newton and son Joshua

Celia A. Traynor

Valerie Pugh

Teri Cannavo & Daughter

Mothers and Grandmothers

War Begins; Coalition Aircraft Attack Iraqi Targets

By Jim Garamone, American Forces Press Service

WASHINGTON, March 19, 2003—Operations to disarm Iraq have begun, President Bush announced during a speech to America tonight.

"On my orders, coalition forces have begun striking selected targets of military importance to undermine Saddam Hussein's ability to wage war," the president said from the Oval Office at 10:15 p.m. Eastern time. Bush stressed this will be a broad and concerted campaign.

—Courtesy of American Forces Press Service

See You Soon

By Bee Pedersen

Bee Pedersen's 19-year-old son Kevin, from the 4th Infantry Division, Fort Hood, Texas, was deployed to Iraq in early April 2003. Bee Pedersen, a native of Denmark, lives in Austin, Texas, with her husband, sons, and two dogs.

We know it's coming. We have known it for quite a while. There's nothing I can do. I'm not in command any longer. I'm out of control. I'm just a spectator and a supplier. My eyes are hurting, and I try to hide that I have been crying. I'm constantly hugging and kissing, hugging and kissing, like a camel accumulating water preparing for a long journey in the desert.

I bury my nose in his hair, a fresh short cut that tickles. I love the smell and try to find a special place in my memory to store it. He tells me not to worry, and I assure him that I don't. Of course I do. He's my son, my baby, and will always be. But I'm strong, I'm a soldier's mom, so I don't cry, and I don't complain.

I don't want him to leave, I don't want to send him in harms way, but it's like a dreaded dentist appointment. The pain while waiting is horrible. You know you have to go, and you want to get it over and done with. I know he feels that way, too. I stay next to him all the time, thinking it's a waste of time to sleep; every moment is precious. We have lunch together. We have dinner together. We talk. We laugh. All the time we both know that we're just trying to get the most out of it.

Several times, for the last few months, we have been called out only for painful false alarms. This time it's for real… my son is going to war. He's going to a foreign country with different traditions, rules, and laws, with its sons and daughters ready to fight for their country.

"My son is going to war...! I repeat it to myself, not believing the words leaving my mouth… "My son is going to war!"

I want to give him something special to carry with him,

something personal, something protective, something to empower, and something to comfort. The last moment, just before he turns around and walks away, I reach for his hand and drop my dad's, (his grandpa's,) old watch into it. I smile at him and nod. We both know that grandpa will watch out for him from the other side.

He calls me from his cell-phone. It's midnight, his dad's birthday. It's time to leave, it's time to say, *"See you soon...!"*

I never say 'goodbye,' because there's no such thing as 'goodbye'. I try to control myself, show him that I'm strong and proud of him. I am. I am so proud of him. My baby, 19 years old, is going to war. I cry inside... *why, why, why*?

For a moment I speculate why it's okay to send him to war when he's not even trusted to drink a beer. The countdown has started, and I don't know what to say or feel. I wish that I could hold him, kiss him, and not let him go, but I can't. I know I won't talk to him for a long time, and in my panic to say the right things, I can only say, *"I love you."*

In a dumpster, close to an airplane heading toward Kuwait, the cell phone's battery is running out. I know that tomorrow morning, I'll put the cell-phone membership on hold... but for how long?

"I'm thinking about how unpatriotic I sound when I talk about my fear, and I know that it is hard for people to understand. I love my country, but I was in elementary school during the Vietnam War and I remember too well the lists of dead soldiers on the news and wearing MIA/POW bracelets. At that time, it never even occurred to me that some day my own son might be involved..."

My Son is Going to War

By Melanie D. Villarreal

One of Melanie Day Villarreal's sons left for Iraq with the 1st Cavalry out of Fort Hood, in January 2004. Another son is on a refueling tanker jet. Melanie D. Villarreal and her husband, Benjamin Villarreal, Jr., are the parents of four sons and one daughter: John, Benjamin, James, Albert and Jennifer. Melanie is currently working as a paralegal in San Saba, and volunteers her time as a flute teacher and guard instructor at Goldthwaite High School.

My son is going to war! My Jimmy is going to a foreign land to fight! A land where teenagers fall upon soldiers and slit their throats, just because they wear American uniforms. Jimmy is going to this place because my President believes he should go... but my President doesn't have a son.

When Jimmy was born, the hospital was short of nurses, so a nurse's aide provided the care for the newborns. She brought me my son and told me what a good baby he was—good because he never cried. She handed me my baby, just hours old, and I saw the waxy, pallid face of a dead person. My son would not stir.

He would not respond. He was dying! My screams echoed through the halls of the old hospital. The nurse's aide just stood there looking at me, not knowing what to do. It was I who called the pediatrician and told him that my son was dying. The doctor was there within minutes. Within the hour, my son was in a neonatal ICU unit. I saved my baby. *Who will save my baby when the Iraqis attack?*

Jimmy joined the Army because he idolizes his grandfather, my father, a World War II and Korean War veteran. My father told Jimmy about the 'glories' of war—not of people dying, but of the mariner with 'a girl in every port.' My father and my grandmother conspired to alter the date on my father's birth certificate, so that he could join the Merchant Marines at the age of seventeen. By his eighteenth birthday, he had sailed around the world. My father told my son about missing his ship and getting stranded in Casablanca for 109 days with no money, and how the generous citizens of Casablanca opened their hearts and their homes to the boy from Texas. My father never told Jimmy about his buddies who died. My father never told Jimmy about sailing into Pearl Harbor and witnessing the devastation left by the Japanese attack. My father has never shown Jimmy the high school yearbook, which bears my father's neatly written notes by the sides of so many pictures of young, hopeful boys. Notes that say things like 'Died at Coral Sea, May, 1942'. Notes that explain why so many of the young men from that dusty little South Texas town never made it to any high school reunions.

I am supposed to be proud of my son. I am expected to wave the flag and tell the world that I believe in what he is doing. I am going to have to tell his brothers and sister that they have nothing to fear when Jimmy leaves with the First Cavalry in January, and then spend every moment I can watching the television, praying that I'll see him alive, praying that he never steps foot on a damned Blackhawk helicopter, hoping that it is not his tank or track vehicle that has become the latest target for Iraqi antitank weapons.

When Jimmy went to basic training at Fort Leonard Wood, he had fallen in love. While he was gone, the girl met someone else and broke off their relationship. A few months ago, Jimmy was the best man at his brother Benjie's wedding. Jimmy gave the toast to the newlyweds. The toast he gave was about how many of his friends had gone off to basic with a special someone in their lives, and how many of those relationships had not survived the separation of basic training. We all knew Jimmy was speaking from his heart about finding true love and looking forward to a future together.

My son is very loving, kind and affectionate. He loves children. He wants to marry and have a big family; he wants to play with his dog; he wants to help his father build things; he wants to do so many things with his life. Please God, watch over him and protect him and bring him home safely to us.

A son, a husband, a brother...
A soldier on a guardpost in Tikrit, Iraq, 2004.

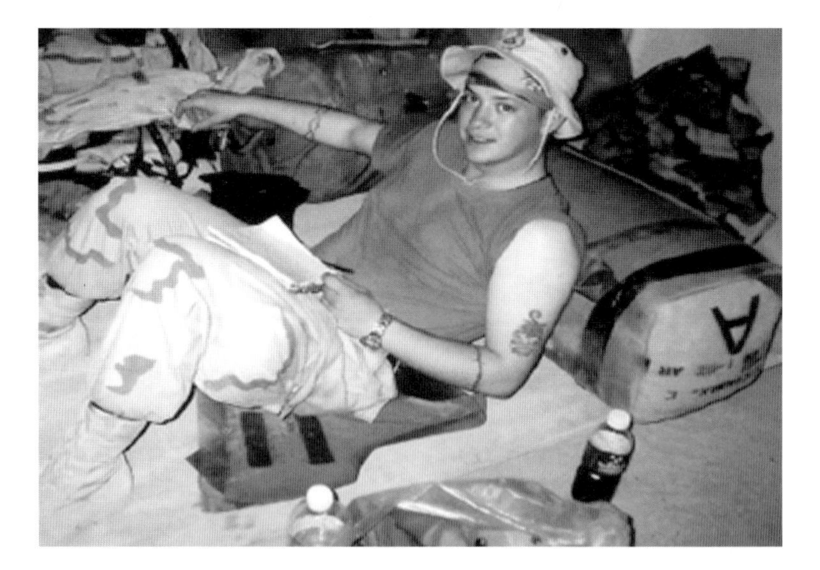

Charlene Sawyer's son, Eric. "He made a promise that he would return home safe, and then he added, 'I don't break a promise.'"

After Food and Water, Troops Want Mail

By Rudi Williams, American Forces Press Service

WASHINGTON, April 8, 2003

French military commander and emperor Napoleon Bonaparte declared that an army travels on its stomach.

That still holds true today, with one important addition: "It's been said that after food and water, the troops want their mail next," said Edward A. Pardini, deputy director, Military Postal Service Agency.

"Mail and packages are extremely important to troops, particularly from family, loved ones and friends," Pardini emphasized

—Courtesy of The American Forces Press Service

It's Just the Angels Stretching Their Wings

By Patti Kiser

Patti Kiser's son was deployed to Iraq, March 2003. Patti Kiser lives in a cabin in Nelchina, Alaska, and has been married 33 years. She has two children, three grandchildren, two dogs, a cat and three chickens. Her son, Sergeant Jacobe Kiser, is with the 4th Military Police Company, 4th Infantry Division

Dear Son,

As I sit in my chair this morning, I am thinking of you. I am wondering if the muscles in my back will ever unclench, or the knot that's in the pit of my stomach will ever relax. Then I think about how you must feel.

You have endured the blazing sun. Having the moisture sucked from your body. Being infested with sand flies. Eating out of cans or packages for months on end. Dealing with rats stealing your food. These are just the simple things you have to deal with: Sleeping outside to just gaze at the stars; the same stars that I gaze upon. You, wishing to be home: I, wishing for your safe return home. Will you ever get used to the bombs, or the sound of bullets in the night? Do you wake with your heart pounding, wondering if you're safe or not? And when a comrade falls, will you get him to safety in time, or will you have to take the loss?

When mail call comes, you are wondering who will write. And of those who didn't, be gentle to them. They just don't understand; maybe do not wish to understand, or simply just turn the other way. But we understand. Way deep inside we have one thought that you may not be coming home. But we push that thought right back where it came from just as fast as we can. And then we think of the things we should have done. We think about the things we will be doing differently now... Life is precious. Hurry home so we can start those precious moments again!

You talked about the children of Iraq, and their sufferings.
Be strong. We Americans come from good stock; we have broad

shoulders and we can carry the load. You are such a magnet to children—they love you, and they can sense it from you.

If I could send you the snow-covered mountains, you know that I would.
If I could send you the crackling fire, you know that I would.
If I could send you a warm fluffy bed, you know that I would.
If I could send you protection, know that I already have.

I talked to my angels and told them not to worry so much about me in my daily life, but to do double duty on you.

Remember the poem we wrote together? You must have been nine or ten. You sent that poem to me a few years ago for my birthday because you couldn't think of what to get that would be special, and mean something. I send it back to you. Kind of our 'heart-to-heart' connection.

Every time we get a letter from you, I let your dog smell it. His tail just starts to wag and he tries to steal it from me. He looks at me with those eyes of his, asking, "Where are you?" "When will you be home?" And I tell him, "It's okay boy; he's coming home soon!" As the tears fall, I just grab onto him, and we will just sit for a while. Then I continue about my day.

I can cry now that you're gone. Saying goodbye was really hard. That was nine months ago. Kids just don't like seeing mom cry. Prepare yourself, 'cause the moment I see your face, it will be like the Hoover Dam breaking loose, 'cause there's gonna be some happy crying going on. And when I look in your eyes, I will see wisdom beyond your years, and pain, and sorrow, and joy ... my kid. I will see a proud man. I love you, son.

"See ya soon." Funny how we all have our little sayings at the close of a letter. Been saying, "See ya soon" for nine months now ... four or less to go…. Hoorah.

P.S. If you see some dust swirling around you, don't worry. It's probably just the angels stretching their wings….

"I have learned that you can catch all of the tears, but you can't keep them from falling."

Surviving At Home

By Janet Witt

Janet Witt and her husband, Rick, live in Cedar Falls, Iowa. They have a daughter, Angela Rooney, a Staff Sergeant in the U.S. Air Force, and a son, Brian, currently a college student. Her daughter served in Iraq during 'Operation Iraqi Freedom'. Janet works as a secretary at the University of Northern Iowa. Her hobbies include sewing, needlework, camping, and gardening.

Veteran's Day weekend, 2002

Our daughter comes home from the Air Force base where she is stationed for a quick weekend visit. A war will surely be starting within weeks or months. She clues us in that she most certainly will be deployed.

January, 2003

We know she's going. We don't know when or where. Later, her phone call lets us know she's arrived, wherever she is. She can't give us much information, but says she's fine, she'll be safe. "Don't worry about me," she adds. Yeah, right. For months, her letters and phone calls are sporadic. As soon as I have an address, I write letters often, wondering when/if she will ever receive them. I lug heavy care packages to the post office. If they'll ever arrive is anybody's guess. Her husband, also in the Air Force, assures us she's okay. We know he knows more than he can tell.

We wait, we wonder, we hope, we pray. I am glued to the TV. CNN is my lifeblood, giving me news on the progress of the impending war. One weekend, we go away with friends. I tell myself it will do me good to get away from the TV. Still, I find myself sneaking glimpses at the hotel TV every chance I get. I cry when I hear reports of soldiers being killed or taken captive. I know that somewhere there's another mother just like me, grieving. When the families of the fallen soldiers are interviewed on national TV, they always sound so strong, so brave. Don't expect me to act like that if anything happens to MY child. I would surely fall apart.

Sometimes our phone rings in the middle of the night. With a nine-hour time difference, I have usually been sleeping for a few hours when she has an opportunity to call. I spring to life. I can wake up quickly when it's important. Just hearing her voice revives me. I can't help wondering what it was like during previous wars when soldiers couldn't phone home. The care and support of friends and family are tremendous. News travels fast. I receive letters, electronic mail messages, and phone calls from people I haven't talked to in months. Everyone wonders what they can do, how they can help. I ask them to pray, and I offer to give them her address. I know more letters will go out in the next day's mail. The local newspaper publishes pictures of local families' loved ones overseas. Extra clippings of her picture appear in our mailbox; sometimes the donor doesn't even identify himself.

A local sign company prints yard signs proclaiming, "We Support Our Troops". They sell out before noon. My name goes on a waiting list for the next batch. The sign stands in our front yard for months. Rain soaks it repeatedly; a windstorm blows it across the street. I snatch it back, patch it together, and put it back up. The flag flies in front of our house every day. All over town, billboards show support. "God Bless America." "Give Our Troops A Hand." More flags go up. The protesters are outnumbered.

Finally, she has access to e-mail. What a relief! No more waiting weeks for our messages to go through. Amazing pictures also arrive. Pictures of a land far away that I know I'll never see. She's seen and done so much more than many of us twice her age.

And then, FINALLY, the news she's that coming home. She's strong, she's safe. I am so proud of her. I told her when she was a child that I knew she could do hard things, but I had no clue this is what her future would hold.

"While it's the duty of every military person to serve their country, perhaps it is the duty of every person left behind to remind others what this side of military life is like."

First Lady Thanks Fort Hood Families

By Donna Miles, American Forces Press Service

WASHINGTON, March 8, 2004

"Today, we celebrate the spirit of another strong group in the military — the elite special forces who don't wear uniforms or fly Black Hawks or carry weapons: a band of sisters who support their loved ones, and each other, so that America remains a land of freedom," she said.

—Courtesy American Forces Press Service

I'm a War Mom

By Sheree Newton

Sheree Newton is the mother of a 22-year-old deployed soldier from the 299 Engineer Battalion, which is attached to the 1st Brigade of the 4th Infantry Division. Sheree Newton, an Operations Analyst for a consulting firm, and her husband of 25 years, Craig, live in Terrell, Texas. They have one child, Joshua, who left for his tour in Iraq, February 5, 2003. Sheree also has two grandchildren: Brooke, six, and Hayden, seven months.

I swear I thought I was ready. I had psyched myself up with positive phrases and, "You can do this!" played over and over in my head. I never had any doubt that I'm a strong woman, and I would always be strong for my family. That all disappeared last February.

In February 2003, my son—my only child—a 22-year-old Army soldier, was deployed to Iraq. He entered the service in February 2002. His father and I were very proud that he was doing something to better himself, and earn college money at the same time. During high school, my son Josh's focus was not on school, sports, or his future.

It was, "where's the next party?" Josh's rebellion cost him a lot of choices for his future. As parents, we fought him every step of the way, but he's rather strong-willed. Eventually, my husband convinced me that we had to let him fall, and fall hard. Only then would he start to see what he needed to do for himself. It took him four-and-a-half years to figure it out. Since his options were limited, he finally saw our advice to go into the military as the only way to go forward.

Josh wanted to be a tanker like his dad had been, but the Army convinced him to be a combat engineer. After completing his basic training at Fort Leonard Wood, Missouri, his first duty station was Fort Hood, Texas. We were so glad he would be near home outside of Dallas, and therefore get to come home on weekends, etc.

Shortly after reporting to Fort Hood, Texas, in August 2002,

Josh married his girlfriend Jeni in a civil ceremony in Killeen, Texas. They didn't tell anyone until two weeks later, and believe me; I was in a state of shock! I kept thinking, "Josh a husband?" But they both surprised me. They were so loving and caring of each other, and I must say I felt relieved that he had someone he loved so much and that they would take care of each other. In December 2002, three months into their marriage, Jeni's pregnancy was announced. Once again, I was surprised, but not shocked.

During all this time, rumors swirled that war would soon be coming as the United States moved forward in its war against terrorism. I swear I heard it everyday that Bush wanted to go to war, but I had faith—faith that it was all just drama—and at the last minute, we wouldn't go to war. But starting in late December and January, the 'noise' of war became louder. Josh called me and said his deployment papers were dated January 31, 2003, but it had been delayed so many times, no one got excited anymore.

After numerous false alarms, we got the word that Josh would be leaving on a ship to escort the vehicles to Iraq the first week of February. I drove to Killeen with Jeni's mom so I could drive Josh's car back to my house. Jeni would move out and back home to her mom's a little later. Seeing their apartment, and the life they were making together made me feel so sad that it would be interrupted. Jeni pregnant, Josh leaving for war, and these two moms were trying to hold it together. Ha! I find it so funny now that I actually even thought I had anything 'together'.

Let me just say this, I *was* strong the day I said 'goodbye' to my son. I spent two days with Josh and Jeni, and when I said goodbye, I was so proud of myself. I had willed myself not to cry. The last thing my son needed was a weeping, hysterical mother hanging on him. He knew I was dying inside as I hugged him, and I almost ran to the car. I don't even remember the 180 miles I drove home that night. But even then, I still thought I was ready.

A couple of weeks go by, life goes on, and you try to pretend that every nerve in your body is not frazzled. You keep praying that this is all a show of force, and that war is not going to happen.

Hey, you almost believe it too! In the meantime, Josh is on a ship, inching closer and closer to danger. Fuzzy memories of 24-hour news channels ... Turkey saying no ... floating around in the Mediterranean Sea, Suez Canal, and clinging to every bit of news you can find. At this point, you start to think, "Well, I may not be as ready as I thought".

Finally, a call from Josh the last week of March! I am thrilled beyond words to hear his voice! The ship he's on is docked in Kuwait and they're waiting for the 4th ID (Infantry Division) to arrive. Josh's unit, the 299 Engineer Battalion, is attached to the 1st Brigade of the 4th ID. He's so hungry for news and information, and we try our best, but we can't tell him what's going on, other than rumors. We tell him that the 4th ID is still at Fort Hood, and this really depresses him. I actually heard my son sound disappointed that the 3rd ID and the Marines would get all the action and it would all be over by the time the 4th ID rolled into Iraq.

I will never understand what the military did to my little boy that made him so ready to go to battle. Yeah sure, he's over 6 feet, 3 inches tall, and one helluva strong, athletically built, good-looking guy—but he is still my little boy. The sweet little guy that brought home every stray animal he found. The six-year-old that screamed from the back seat when he saw a turtle crossing a road and made his dad stop and pick it up. When they opened the trunk of the car, the turtle was not in the box they placed him in. He had vanished! Well, not really. He crawled up behind the back seat where he fell in the body of the car and died. After a few sweltering days in Texas, use your imagination as to how the car smelled. This little boy who accidentally shot the side of my new refrigerator with a BB gun—this sweet baby of mine—was ready to go to war and kill.

I struggled with that knowledge. Josh was not afraid. On the phone, I would listen for any hesitation or waffling, but no, he was ready to go. I'm not sure what I would have done if I had sensed fear in him. I was dizzy with helplessness and my instinct to protect him; knowing full well I could not. So my son gave me a precious gift. Every time we got to speak on the phone, his words and manner let me know he was not afraid. His training kept him so focused on the battle that there was no fear at all, only frustration because his unit was not there. But they got there the first week of April, and I estimated that Josh and his unit crossed into Iraq, from Kuwait, on or about April 12th or 13th.

The day the war started, I was at work. I remember CNN was on in the break room and quite a few people gathered around with solemn faces. I sat at my desk weeping uncontrollably. I have never been so afraid in all my life. People I work with would walk by my desk and notice this woman sobbing, and I saw the pity in their eyes. People just trying to ask a question about my son, or even just trying to offer comfort, sent me into a crying spell that would last anywhere from a few minutes to hours. All I can say is that I had the physical feeling of spiraling out of control with pain and fear. Now this is the first day of the war and my son's still in Kuwait on a boat, and I'm an emotional blubbering idiot. My husband and I both sat in front of the television every minute we were home trying to get as much information as possible. We were pretty much on TV overload by the first week, but I couldn't stop. This is the only way I can feel even remotely close to my son, and I'm not taking my eyes off it until I can't keep them open any longer. So I am rolled up in a blanket on the couch and staring at the tube. There was nothing else I could do. I knew for a certainty that I was ready for nothing.

On May 1st, I did what Vivi, in the *Divine Secrets of the YaYa Sisterhood* described best. I "dropped my basket". Up until that day, I had been to the doctor several times since the war started, complaining of symptoms almost identical to menopause. Two different doctors told me my physical symptoms were the result of extreme stress and agitation. My focus at work was gone; I couldn't remember anything from day-to-day. The days were strung together in a blur of pain, so I was put on antidepressants. That seemed to help for a little while, but on May 1, George Bush went on television and declared major combat over in Iraq. I sat in front of the TV stunned! "What the hell did he just say? Are you kidding me?"

My mind must not have been able to cope, and I felt myself

spinning again. A few beers later, and replaying the presidents words over and over in my mind... I began to scream inside.... The president just made damn sure our soldiers still there would more or less be forgotten by a large majority of the American public. It was pretty bad when I saw pity in the eyes of people who found out, or already knew where Josh was, but to announce major combat over was taking the war off the radar for most people. In fact, Josh asked me soon after if the soldiers over in Iraq had been forgotten by the American people. Of course, my reply was, "Not with my big mouth out here."

I will admit to being almost weary with it all. My work has suffered, as well as my personal life. The people I work with and my family are tired of hearing my newest information, etc. I'm positive most of them feel I'm obsessed with my son and the war. Maybe I am, but it's the only way I know how to cope and feel useful. It's so hard, and I feel alone much of the time. The only time I don't feel alone is when I go to the 4th Infantry Division Association website and "share" with others like me. I happened on the site back in April, and it's been a Godsend. I can't remember all the details, but one woman posted that if your loved one was a member of the 4th ID, go to this site and get on the Forum. I can't remember a day when I haven't logged on and read, or posted on the board. This is the place for support. The Vietnam vets, who the site belongs to, were stunned that they had suddenly been overrun with a bunch of women asking questions like "package size" requirements to Iraq; what do I send my soldier; has anyone heard from the 299 Engineer Battalion? You name it, it's pretty much been posted, and it can get hysterically funny or make you mad enough to spit nails, but it feels like home. When I have happy news to report, like when my grandson was born, or Josh got to come home for two weeks of R&R in October, I post it here, and my new family offers congratulations and well wishes.

Other times when it's sad news, the wonderful support and well wishes pull you through a bad time. It truly is the 'soft place to fall' that everyone should have. I have typed through many tears on this bulletin board, and made what I hope to be lifelong friends. The vets have turned into the most wonderful and knowledgeable sources of information you could ask for. They tell us the truth, and for the most part, are big brothers to us. Now that doesn't mean that the 'family fight' doesn't break out every now and then. There have been more fights and altercations than I care to remember, but no one got hurt, and it makes for some interesting reading, if not a really hard belly laugh! When Josh was home on leave, I asked him to type a 'hello' in there and he did. He was a little shy, but when he read the wonderful response from all the 'gang' he asked, "Mom, how did you meet these people? They are great!" Made me feel proud of my new friends and the way they rallied to welcome my son home. Yes, I told my son, we are a weird cult. 'The Oldest Cheerleaders in the World' cult! Cheering our loved ones in Iraq and each other is what we do.... No one would pay us, but we're priceless. Just don't get us started on how our pom-poms look.

I spoke earlier of the danger in Josh's job, and can only say that if I had been with him when he enlisted, I would not have let him pick that Military Occupational Specialty. This unit is the first in. That means they secure the area for the other soldiers behind them. They clear mines, blow up ammunition and pretty much anything else that's asked of them. I can't believe I thought a combat engineer built bridges and mostly did contracting type work. I guess I put it out of mind and came back to it later, because in August, I dropped my basket again. I won't go into detail, but let's just say I drank too much, probably made a fool of myself, and heard the pity in the voice of more than one person.

Josh had called me and told me about riding in a convoy, and the truck in front of his hit a mine on the side of the road. He said a female was driving, and the explosion blew her straight out the left side and onto the ground, but the soldier in the passenger seat was blown straight up and came down. Josh said they ran up to help. The female was in shock, and all she asked was, "How do I look?" Josh informed me that she wanted him to tell her if she had all her limbs still attached. He told her she looked fine, and then the medics took over. He ran over to the male soldier and saw right away that one of his legs was blown off. He said he got really nauseous, but kept the guy talking until they could airlift him out of there. Josh gave me his name and asked me if I could find out what happened to him.

Well, low and behold, Bob Babcock's daily update came on that Saturday and had an article about the sheer number of soldiers coming through Walter Reed Hospital. He then went on to describe the actual injuries sustained in Iraq by our soldiers. I was stunned! The soldier Josh asked me to check on was in the article, and he had lost a leg. He would live, but he was just one of thousands who had life-changing injuries. Amputations, burns, loss of sight; the list went on and on. Once again, I started to hear the screaming inside! Oh my God!! I went into only what I can describe as a frantic state of weeping and praying for my kid to come home the way he left. I was ashamed of myself for not paying more attention and trying to understand exactly what it meant when I heard someone was injured.

The fear that took hold of me was nauseating and left me stunned. I have worked hard since that time to get a better hold of my emotions and be a part of my daily life again. I want to be the mother my son remembers when he gets home, and not a fragile wreck. I have started to move to more positive thoughts again, and days when I don't, I just keep going forward. One day at a time, ever hopeful that this will all have a happy ending. I want to grow old watching my son and his family thrive. As I sit here tonight watching my grandson sleep, I see his father and I smile. God took care of me when he gave me this little boy to love… both times.

"I have come to realize that there are worse things than war. Living in a world where there is nothing worth fighting for, or worth protecting, is by far, more devastating than any war the world has known."

Staff Sergeant Angela Rooney and comrades in front of a Blackhawk. Iraq, 2003. “For months, letters and phone calls are sporadic. ‘Don’t worry about me,’” she adds.

Sherri Martin’s daughter, Julie, holding on to her daddy’s leg before he goes back to Iraq after R&R.

Myers Charts Coalition Military Actions to Date

By Jim Garamone, American Forces Press Service

WASHINGTON, March 21, 2003—American ground forces are 100 miles inside Iraq and driving on Baghdad, Chairman of the Joint Chiefs of Staff, Air Force Gen. Richard Myers, said today during a Pentagon news conference.

The U.S. air campaign against Saddam Hussein's regime began with a tremendous bombing campaign against military targets against Baghdad, Kirkuk and Mosul, he said.

—Courtesy American Forces Press Service

My Story

By Renate "Rain" Nietzold

Two of Renate Nietzolds' five kids and her daughter-in-law are deployed to Iraq. "Rain" is a 50-year-old Army Mom. She lives in the Chicago area and owns and publishes a motorcycle magazine for women called 'Biker Ally Magazine'. Her son, Shawn Carter, stepson Robert (Bobby) Nietzold, and his wife, Christina Nietzold, are all deployed to Iraq.

My name is Renate Nietzold, known to most as simply, 'Rain'. I was born in Germany, and I immigrated to America with my parents. I made my citizenship, and I am very proud to be an American, something that has been passed on to my children. I am the mom of five kids. Two (a boy and a girl) are my own, and three are my stepsons. My own son, Shawn Carter, age, 21, is with the Headquarters and Headquarters Company, 1/8 Infantry, 4th Infantry Division out of Fort Carson, Colorado and stationed in Balad. My middle son, Robert (Bobby) Nietzold, age 22, is with the 3rd Infantry as a military policeman out of Fort Stewart, Georgia, and stationed in Baghdad. He is married, and his wife, Christina Nietzold, is also with the 3rd Infantry currently stationed in Kuwait. Now that you have a brief history, here is my story....

The year was 2002, and for me, this was going to be a great holiday. Our entire family was going to be together under one roof. The only downside of this Christmas was that we knew our military people were going to be deployed to Iraq soon. It was nice to spend time with all the kids, and none of us wanted to think about what was going to happen in the near future. I was able to say goodbye to my son Bobby and his wife at our house as he was driving back to his base. My other son Shawn was being driven to the airport. Because of the 9/11 incidents, we were unable to spend any time at the airport. With a quick hug and kiss, my son was out of sight before I could even get adjusted to him being gone. Emptiness had already begun to set in for what would prove to be just the beginning of my own personal turmoil. On January 15, 2003, we received a call from Bobby telling us that he was going to be shipping out to Iraq in one week. Concern over his safety was the first thing on everyone's mind. We had been glued to the TV, and knew that we would now and forever have this as an attachment until our sons returned.

I was scheduled for a hysterectomy on April 2. I knew that my other son Shawn would be leaving any day, and was really hoping that it wouldn't be happening during my hospital stay. I went under the knife with many concerns, and woke up with two units of blood missing, as well as being handed a phone. My son was on the other end saying, "Mom, I hope you are all right and I really hate telling you this, especially this way, but I'm looking at my plane and have to get on board to Iraq."

I was under medication and really didn't want to hear about his deployment like this. Another pain in my heart developed, and another bout of misery came upon me.

In June of 2003, my daughter-in-law handed us the news of her deployment to Kuwait. She said more than likely she would not be seeing any type of action and would just be doing missions into Iraq. She had been keeping us informed of Bobby's whereabouts, and his mental, as well as his physical condition. With all three in Iraq now—we, like other parents, spouses, and siblings—sit and await any news at all. I guess this is the hardest thing to do. For us, every phone call could be one of them; the TV hasn't left our sight, and our ears perk up with any mention of Iraq. I wait impatiently for the mail to come, in hopes of getting a letter. Recently, I've been leaving my e-mail account opened to see if any messages come in, as both boys now have e-mail access.

Bobby and Christina do not write often. In fact, if we get one letter a month we are blessed. A phone call comes in about as often, but at least we hear from them and know that they are all right. Each time I have spoken with Bobby, I have heard shooting in the background, and this gets me pretty freaked out.

"Don't worry, they are pretty far away," says Bobby. His whole outlook on the Iraqi situation is this: "Iraq is a pretty dangerous place, but I'm upholding the law and arresting a lot of criminals."

One of Bobby's best friends got shot in the arm and leg, and he was returned to the States. If it weren't for Bobby taking out the bad guys, neither he nor his friend would have survived the day. While on patrol, he lost another friend during an attack. This friend was a machine gunner and got hit with a fatal bullet from a sniper.

Bobby finds it increasingly difficult to deal with the loss and injuries that his friends receive. Depression is hard for him. To make matters worse, he cannot seem to get in touch with his wife, and is concerned over her welfare as well. The first question from him is always, "Have you heard from Christina?" Most of the time my answer is 'No'. I feel helpless that there's nothing I can do, not even give him a little bit of information about his wife.

Shawn, on the other hand, loves to write. There isn't a week that goes by that I don't receive at least two letters. His calls have been coming in very frequently, and I enjoy each and every one of them. He also e-mails us, and we hear from him at least once a week. I am amazed over this because Shawn happens to be dyslexic, and writing and reading has always been somewhat of a chore for him. Where Bobby informs us of everything that's going on, Shawn does not. He keeps everything to himself and doesn't want to talk about anything that is happening with him. All he wants to know is what's going on at home. Shawn is very homesick, but still has a very good outlook on life, and has been able to maintain his sense of humor. Anyone else would say he's fine. As his mom, I know better. I know that he has seen more things than anyone can imagine. I get the subtle hints and pick up on his missing words. I can only offer support, understanding and caring, while I fall apart on the inside.

Shawn did relay one incident. He was on a convoy, and the truck in front of him got hit with a missile. He saw one of his friends injured. His job was to provide cover while they worked on his friend. After a long while of fighting and exchanging bullets, everyone else made it out of there in one piece. His friend lost a leg as a result, but is glad that the rest of the unit was able to pull him out of the situation.

When my sons tell me of these kinds of incidents, I can only think, "It could have easily been him." Of course, then I realize this is a selfish thought, but I'm sure everyone who has heard this type of stuff thinks the same thing. "I'm glad it wasn't my son, but I'm so sorry that someone else did get hurt." It almost makes you feel guilty.

I wish I could go to Iraq and take their place. I'm proud of them, and they have grown up so much in the last couple of months. I wish they could have grown up under different circumstances. They are too young, just as all the soldiers were during the Vietnam times. This war is a little different than Vietnam, but in many ways it is the same.

My life has become an emotional roller coaster. This war has changed me as well. I pray for everyone's safe return, and the time of his or her target homecoming can't come soon enough. I feel as if I can't control my emotions, even though everyone says I'm holding up rather well. They don't see the downside of me; not even my husband can see what I'm really going through. I remain the rock of the family. When I'm alone, I cry and ask why. Why does this world have to be like it is? Why can't we just get along? I personally don't think I'm coping; I'm falling apart, torn between my patriotic duty and that of being a mother. I want to bring back the time when they were young: I surely haven't given them enough hugs and kisses. I wish I could go back, but all I can do is go forward into the unknown. There isn't a day that passes by that I don't shed a tear. I'm lost and out of control. For me, that's the hardest thing—being out of control. I'm a person of action and a person who gets things done, problems solved. I can't solve this, and I feel like screaming at the top of my lungs about the unfairness of it all.

My heart goes out to all those who have been wounded and their families. My heart breaks over any news of any soldier that's been killed, and I wish I could do something to help their families. But I can't, and life goes on. A short blurb on the TV, a newspaper article, just doesn't seem enough for those that have given so much.

Being the mom of a soldier is Hell! Plain and simple, direct and to the point. There isn't a word or a sentence that can relate to what each of us feel that has a soldier facing danger at every turn—but all of us can relate, all of us have the same feelings. We can't put it into words and do justice to what we feel inside, and what our thoughts are. It must be too personal, too hard for us to deal with. That's the only answer I can come up with. The natural order of things is for us to depart this world first, and we face every day with the unknown and wonder if this order will be broken.

I know that I'm not the only one who looks outside to see if the person knocking at the door is an official-looking person or not, and always hope that he or she isn't. I've become afraid of the unknown. At least when I receive a call, I know that for the moment, they are safe. I've gone to living one day at a time, just getting through each day and hoping that I get some news that day. I've almost made home a prison for myself, never wanting to leave, just in case a call might come in. I force myself to go to work. For me, that's really hard, as I travel a lot with my job, and that means I'm away from home for long periods of time. I've missed many phone calls while traveling, but know that at least my husband is there to answer and relate all that was said.

I recently visited Fort Carson, and had a chat with Shawn's commanding officer's wife. We got into a light debate over who misses their soldier more, a mom or a wife. I listened to everything she had to say, and understood where she was coming from. My only comment was this:

"Being a husband and a wife is something that happens through love that is found. From the day that you meet, and from the day you marry, you work on your relationship; it's a constant effort. In today's times, there is no guarantee that it will work and last. Being a mom, struggling to bring forth a life, a part of her, and the love that comes from that, is something that's unconditional. It will never disappear, and it never has to be worked at. It's forever." She saw my point, and told me that I won that argument hands down. Not an argument as far as I'm concerned, just a fact.

Our current situation is that our daughter-in-law may be coming home in December. For that we are very thankful, and cannot wait to see her. However, both of my sons will probably not be coming home until April at the earliest. Both of them had a chance at the mid-tour leave, and both had opted out of the line to come home. They would rather complete their tour and have more time once they're stateside. Both expressed the desire to be home, but both felt that returning to Iraq would be that much harder. Even though they said that they are really homesick and that seeing family and friends would help them a lot, they felt that others needed to be home more. However, both said that those who have gone home on a two-week leave have come back almost bragging ... and that part is so very hard for them to deal with. It's fine that they were able to see their loved ones, but in their opinion, it's not fine to rub it in. It almost makes them wish they hadn't given up their spot. The only thing I could say to that was if they had been home, they would probably be talking about it as well. I told them that I was sure these people didn't mean to rub it in, and that they don't mean to make anyone sad. They're just happy. To that they can only say, "Yes, but it still upsets us that we have remained behind."

Am I jealous over those that returned home? No, I'm glad that some of our soldiers had that opportunity. Do I wish mine were home? Yes, even if it's only for a short while. Then I think about their having to return to Iraq, and I feel that I would probably be one of those who just couldn't deal with that, and find myself glad that they aren't coming back for a brief visit. If they were, I would probably never let them go.

What is the one thing that upsets me the most? I've been asked that time and again. My answer? I live on a block that doesn't show any type of patriotism. I am the only one with yellow ribbons on my tree. My flag hangs each and every day from my house. My service flag has faded long ago. I know that people lead their own lives and don't really stop to think about our soldiers until they see me. Then they ask if I'd heard anything, and never really listen to what I'm saying. They ask me for their address; some have asked at least ten times. I have to wonder why they ask, as they don't ever write them. I get a typical phrase like, "I've been meaning to write." Why bother saying anything like that if you have no intention of writing? They don't have to pacify me. They can do what they want, but they shouldn't pretend to really care. That's what disappoints me the most. I guess I'm just upset that the general public has not kept our military in their thoughts. They only think about them when it hits home. I guess it's human nature, and those of us who do have soldiers facing danger are really the only ones who never have them far from our thoughts.

The best thing about this war is the number of people I have come to know, even if I've never met them. The daily updates we receive, along with what everyone talks about, have helped me a lot. I'm glad to see I wasn't the only person to feel the way I did. It made me realize that there are a lot of people out there experiencing the same thing—some like me for the first time; others have been through this more than once. The best quotation that I've heard to date and one that I use frequently is, "Tears on my pillow, pride in my heart." This alone sums up everything, and this alone keeps me going. I'm sorry to say I don't know the origin of this saying, but my hat is off to its creator!

The Tigris River, Iraq

A Broken Marriage and Hurt Feelings

By Charlene Sawyer

Charlene Sawyer's son, Eric, is with the 4th Infantry Division and was deployed to Iraq in April 2003. Charlene and husband Tim have three children, Eric, Timothy, and Jennifer. She is also mom to stepdaughter, Shanay. Charlene works at Rubbermaid in Canton, Ohio.

My son, Eric, is in the Army with the 4th Infantry Division, and he left in April with his group to go to Iraq. In February, prior to his deployment, his wife had left him. Obviously, my son had this on his mind and so he left me 'power of attorney' to deal with all his legal problems.

The first thing my son wanted me to do was to file for divorce, but his wife wouldn't sign the dissolution. They had only been married eight months and owned nothing.

I am very proud of my son, and the fact that he is doing a difficult and dangerous job keeping our country safe. When he writes me, he tells me how bad it is over there. The weather is over 130 degrees, and he has been sick a lot because of that. You see, their equipment weighs more than 50 pounds and sometimes they have to wear it all day. My son really doesn't go into details, but I do know how bad it is. Every day I listen to the TV or radio and I hear of soldiers dying. It just makes me sick! Before my son left, he made me a promise: a promise that he would return home safe, and then he added, "I don't break a promise!"

Understandably, my son is going through a lot of stress and anger right now. I had to tell him that his wife used her 'power of attorney', that was no good anymore, to withdraw all but $10 of savings from the bank. My son really needs to focus on what he is doing in Iraq, but it is hard for him to do so.

My son and an ex-girlfriend have a child together, and she had learned that he was making extra money, so she wanted her child support to be modified. I received a letter from my son who was pretty upset because he had received legal papers in Iraq, with the court date, to get the child support modified. Because of the time it takes mail to reach Iraq, he did not receive these papers until after the court date, and so they took it upon themselves to have his child support modified. I think it is a travesty that our government's military and legal systems would allow a mate of our sons and daughters who are fighting a war to file legal proceeding papers. This requires that the son, or daughter, be present or default (lose). How in the world can they be present when they are in a country fighting for freedom? Shouldn't the number one priority be to keep their mental status as positive as possible so they remain alert to the danger they're facing? Shouldn't their attention be on keeping themselves, their fellow patriots, and innocent people they're protecting, alive and safe? How can they do that when they are presented with legal problems back home they aren't capable of handling? How was this tragic loophole overlooked for our proud fighting men and women of the U.S.A.?

I cannot believe what people would do to get that extra dollar, and the legal system should have known that it takes three or four weeks to get mail to our soldiers, sometimes even longer.

With everything going on with my son, it has caused him to be very depressed, and his morale is very low. That doesn't make it easy for him to concentrate on protecting himself and people in Iraq. So whatever my son is feeling, I feel the same. I feel the anger as much as he does. I just cannot wait until they come home and all this is over.

"It is now May 17th and still no word from our son, Jackson. The waiting is truthfully unbearable; it seems as if they all have disappeared from the surface of this planet. You don't even hear about the soldiers on the news like before. This war is not over till our soldiers are home!"

Renate Nietzold's son, Shawn, with Iraqi children.

Curlen M. Martinson on an Iraqi tank, Iraq, 2003.

"As a mother, nurse, and officer in the United States Air Force, It is not always easy understanding the whys and the hows."

Walk Away into Danger

By Teri Cannavo

Teri Cannavo's son, 21-year-old son, Private First Class Dustin Patterson, is a tank driver with HHC 1-67 Armor. He went into Iraq, April 8, 2003. He graduated from boot camp, Jan. 19, 2003, but had already received deployment orders by Jan. 13, 2003. Teri Cannavo and her husband Carl reside in Las Vegas, Nevada, where she works in a grocery store. She has two children: Dustin, and her nine-year-old daughter, Lacie.

My son went back to Iraq Monday night. He had been home on a two week R&R. It was so nice to have him home and to not have to worry too much. The relief I felt was weird ... haven't felt that decent in a year. He had a good time, saw lots of friends and family. And yes, we did try to squeeze too much into too little time, but he was able to spend lots of his hard-earned money. (My son is single, so he didn't have any obligations. Lucky for him, eh?) Anyway, so now my husband and I find each other with $600 worth of new Play Station games, tons of new dirty clothes on his bedroom floor, and a snake. Not just any snake—it's 'camo' colored, matching his battle dress uniform. (BDUs)

I am so glad we were able to see him, and I know a lot of you have not been able to see your loved ones yet, but let me fill you in on something. I am not complaining; I loved having him home, but the hardest thing I have ever had to do is put him back on that plane and send him back to Iraq.

When my son left the first time last year, we didn't really know what to expect, but now, we know exactly what we are sending our child into. We had some tears, but we painted on game faces, and stood strong. When he hugged his little sister, and they both started to cry, I had to turn away. Usually it's he who is consoling her, so watching both my kids in tears was too much. I left them alone for a minute and then reminded them that he'd be home really soon.

I told him if his Sergeant Major saw him like this, he'd never hear the end of it. He agreed. So he packed all his stuff on his back, and started the long walk down the hallway to the gates.

We watched him walk, alone, all by himself, until we couldn't see him any longer, and the tears were rolling. I think my heart is still somewhere between the parking garage and the A-gates. You feel so helpless, watching them walk away into danger.

As we turned around to leave, there stood another young soldier going back to Iraq. After he had hugged his wife, I told her that my son had just left to go to the gates. She and I cried together, and I told her they would be okay, that our two soldiers were no longer alone. It made us feel better.

He needed this break, but it had a bittersweet taste. We were glad to have it!

GOD BLESS OUR TROOPS!

"Combat stress changes people. It's a pain deep down inside that never seems to go away."

Company C, 3rd Platoon, 1/22nd Infantry, Tikrit, Iraq, 2004
A pyramid of young men with hopes and dreams for their future.

Veteran's Day 2003

By Celia A. Traynor

Celia A. Traynor's son is deployed to Iraq. Celia and husband Paul reside in Huntsville, Alabama, with the two youngest of their four children. She is a homemaker, artist, and lay minister. Her son, David, is a medic with the 4th Infantry Division in Iraq.

My son is in Balad, Iraq, now. The only one in my family that I know who has ever served in a war. Yet I know God protects him. He is in the only city of the "Sunni Triangle" (as the media likes to call it) that isn't Sunni Muslim. It is a Shiite city. They are one of the most cooperative groups in Iraq because of the persecution they saw during the dictatorship.

I think of David and the other soldiers enduring hardship—fighting a most devilish enemy that is both ruthless and cowardly—for the righteous cause of liberty. Freedom: an inalienable right God gave to all mankind when He gave us free will, the ability to choose, the ability to believe. I think of them, the soldiers, and wonder about my own strength. They fight an enemy that seems to hate life. Theirs is a physical conflict, but the conflict or competition, if you will, is still a fight for the minds of men and women. Also, this is a fight within their own minds, to keep their resolve that victory is the only viable outcome. They must be, and they must stay, mentally strong and fully convinced of prevailing in their mission.

As I go through my day-to-day routine, if it starts to get hectic, or become agitated, I try to keep things in perspective. I live in a comfortable home with air conditioning and heat, hot and cold water ... all the modern conveniences. I can get in my car and drive to the store for whatever I need without any concern that I might run into an Improvised Explosive Device along the way.

I think of Proverbs 24:10: *If thou faint in the day of adversity, thy strength is small.*

My son wrote to me about his mental battle to stay positive and believe in his circumstances. He said, "I am fighting the good fight, and I am winning." I want to be like him. I want my strength to be great, and not faint in adversity. I want to keep my thoughts in check and have a prevailing outcome in day-to-day situations. I thank God for showing me how to fight the good fight and win.

"I just watched CNN—it's devastating... 17 soldiers killed. I am deeply saddened and my heart and prayers go out to the families. More than 400 soldiers have died since March. Way too many! God bless our troops!"

US Soldiers Foot Patrol
"The friends we make here are ones to last a lifetime. Friends are your backbone when you think you can't stand anymore."

Bush Pays Surprise Thanksgiving Visit to Troops in Iraq

By Mike Allen, Washington Post Staff Writer

Thursday, November 27, 2003; 4:02 PM —Bush surprised 600 soldiers of the 1st Armored Division and the 82nd Airborne Division attending a Thanksgiving celebration at the Bob Hope Dining Facility on the makeshift military base at Baghdad International Airport, telling them they "are defeating the terrorists here in Iraq so we don't have to face them in our own country."

Happy Thanksgiving
By Patti Kiser

Patti Kiser's son was deployed to Iraq in March 2003. Patti Kiser lives in a cabin in Nelchina, Alaska, and has been married 33 years. She has two children, three grandchildren, two dogs, a cat and three chickens. Her son, Sergeant Jacobe Kiser, is with the 4th Military Police Company, 4th Infantry Division.

Dear Son,
Happy Thanksgiving,

It was a good thing that you called this morning after looking at the news. I won't worry so much today knowing that you are safe, at least for today.

As I sit at the table this morning, drinking my cup of coffee and waiting for the sun to come up over the trees, I think of what it would be like if you were here. I think that you would still be sleeping, waiting for the smell of bacon cooking. Then you might think about getting up. Or you might be asking if I am going to cook pancakes too, and will they have blueberries in them. Yes to all the questions.

I can see you in your baggy shorts, thinking you are too skinny. You look just like your father back when I first met him. You told me the other day how much you weigh, and to me, it wasn't very much at all. The thought that I weigh more than you is a bit scary for me, since I am a lot shorter than you. I know that you are eating well now. Getting three meals a day. And that today you had lobster and turkey. If anyone stateside wants to complain about how well you are eating, they better not say it to my face. To think that you put your life on the line everyday and that you have eaten worse. I say, "Let them take your place for a while and see how they like it."

I think now that you have had breakfast, that you will be calling your friends to meet up for some horseback riding, and I won't see you for the rest of the day. I will miss you not being here today, to sit down around the table and tell us stories about today's riding.

On who got stuck, or how badly someone missed the jump, or who crashed a good one. So as we sit down today with an empty chair, we will think about you and our hearts will swell up with pride. And we know that you want to be here too. I am so glad you called this morning. I will think while we are eating that, right now, you are safe and sleeping....

Did I mention it is 26 degrees below this morning? Even the birds aren't too excited about coming by this sunny morning, and the ones that have, had frost on their heads. They are brave souls this morning. Just like you. You are a brave soul every minute of every day. I thank you, my son.

We have that picture of you on the computer. You know, the one where you are in the desert with the huge goggles on that take up half your face, but, there is that Brad Pitt smile like grandma says you have. It makes me smile too every time I see it. I will go out of my way sometimes just to see that smile. Not like we don't have pictures of you everywhere around the house. The refrigerator is getting full. I can imagine, so is everyone else's around this world that has a son or daughter away from home. Did you get the picture of the caribou on the road we took yesterday? All I could think about was how tasty they would be. We stopped the truck and I was sitting out on the window, and they just stood there. Curious creatures they are, and, it would have been the perfect shot. Ha ha.

We love you. Stay safe, see ya soon.

P.S. Do you think angels need to sleep too? I don't know, but I can see one sitting on the edge of your bed, maybe taking a break till you wake....

"Yeah! Finally I received an e-mail from my hubby! I was so thrilled! At last the Internet is up and running in Baqubah. Yeah!!! My hubby is doing well. I just wanted to share my wonderful news with everyone."

Bee Pedersen's son, Kevin, and fellow soldiers in Iraq, 2003.
"I repeat to myself, not believing the words leaving my mouth... 'My son is going to war!'"

Lori Burling's boyfriend, Jimmy, and a fellow soldier in Kuwait.
"Babe, I don't have a lot of time right now because we all have to use the phone tonight.... Four hours later President Bush told the nation that our military was attacking Iraq."

Tragedy During Iraqi War Brings Mothers Together

By Rudi Williams, American Forces Press Service

WASHINGTON, Oct. 6, 2003 —Tragedy brought Becky Lalush and Millie C. Williams together. They didn't know each other until after their sons were killed together in a helicopter accident in Iraq on March 30.

They live hundreds of miles apart, but Lalush, of Troutville, Va., and Williams, of Port Charlotte, Fla., are finding comfort in leaning on each other as they try to cope with the sudden loss of their sons. They're the first two mothers who lost children during the war in Iraq to join a group of older women called the American Gold Star Mothers, most of whom lost children during the Vietnam War.

—Courtesy American Forces Press Service

I Thought I Knew

By Bee Pedersen

Bee Pedersen's 19-year-old son Kevin, from the 4th Infantry Division, Fort Hood, Texas, was deployed to Iraq in early April 2003. Bee Pedersen, a native of Denmark, lives in Austin, Texas, with her husband, sons, and two dogs.

I thought I knew what it would feel like. I had watched so many movies and listened to so many stories ... stories and movies where even I had been crying. I had related and felt the deep pain and anxiety.... Hollywood had shown me the true picture, right...? So how could I be so mistaken? But I was. I was so mistaken, because I had absolutely no idea what it meant to have a loved one, my son, at war.

You see, I grew up in Denmark, far away from the USA, where war was almost taboo; something that would be going on far away from our borders; something which didn't influence our daily life too much, unless we were demonstrating and put behind bars, as during the Vietnam War. Well, my dad and my grandpa went to war; they served during the 1st and the 2nd World Wars. More than a hundred times I have listened to their stories with terror in my eyes ... horrifying stories about persecutions, concentrations camps, hunger, and death; so, I thought I knew. So tell me my friend, how could I be so mistaken?

I speculate, why am I going through this? Why did my son choose to join the Army? I keep questioning *why*, why me? Is this some kind of a test, and if so, what am I to learn from it?

I wake up in the morning, still feeling tired after eight hours of restless sleep. Reaching for the remote control, I'm starting my suicidal morning routine. The perfectly well-dressed news reporter greets me, telling me in a compassionate and yet professional voice that a helicopter has crashed and 16 soldiers have been killed.

I'm paralyzed and the sunny beautiful morning all of a sudden turns into thick darkness. I search on websites, I listen to every news program on every channel. Every moment I am alert, and the devastating news is running through my home like a cold wind the entire day. *Where was it*? *Did anybody survive*? *Where is my son*? *When will I know that he's okay*? For the next 24 hours, I'll dread any phone call, any activation of my doorbell. I'm like a trembling zombie. I can't think, I can't concentrate, and I can't even perform the most normal daily activities....

I'm paralyzed. I feel empty and so alone, and then I feel like screaming in an attempt to awaken the entire world.... *Have you all forgotten? Are you aware of what's going on*? *Are your lives just continuing as if nothing has happened*? *How can you be so blind*? *How can you just ignore the situation and turn the TV on and off as you please*? You see, it doesn't stop; the cruelty; the sorrow; the anger; the dream and hope of peace ... because you turn off the TV. War isn't a TV movie... it's real, it's my son, it's our sons and daughters fighting, getting wounded and killed... have you thought about that?

I thought I knew... so how could I be so mistaken....

My closet has been turned into a field kitchen loaded with pepperoni sticks, Gatorade powder, beef jerky, jelly beans, baby wipes, mosquito repellent, and much more. Only the day before, I had marched up and down each aisle in the grocery store, trying to figure out what would last a four-to-seven weeks journey to a country with 140 degree heat. It isn't the first time. As a matter of fact, my grocery shopping is turning into a constant search for new, tasteful, robust, and exciting items to send to Iraq. I'm searching up and down, and every time someone questions my search, I take the opportunity to tell him or her about my son. They listen politely, and say they will pray for my son, they tell me how proud I must be, and assure me that they understand how difficult it is. I pretend I'm strong; I look down whenever tears are shaped in the corner of my eyes. How would they know? Sure I'm proud, but I'm so scared too.

I make my first trip to the post office, praying that I have chosen the right goodies. It's weird. I recall when I, as a Girl Scout at camp, would receive goodies from *my* mom. I remember how much that meant to me, and so, I just can't imagine what it will mean to my son in war. When the postal worker asks me where the package is going, I can hardly speak.

"Oh... it's an APO address," he says, and sends me a comforting smile, but still with a teasing glimpse in his eyes. "Any homemade cookies in there?"

Everybody in the room can spot that this is a special package, embroidered with cheering slogans and loving words. I spot another box similar to mine, and looking up, I'm facing the carrier. The woman smiles, "My son is from the 4th ID." "

So is mine," I almost cry with joy. I have found someone who truly understands my pride, my anxiety, my hope, and prayers.

Every day, like a hungry tiger waiting for its prey, I'm look out the window, hoping to spot the funny white car delivering my usual load of mail. Before April 4, it had only been a tedious task going through the meaningless stack of papers, but now the job had suddenly gained a new and special meaning. I'm wishing and hoping that I'll find a small, dirty envelope without stamps ... that I'll receive just a few words from my son. Just four small words: "I'm doing fine, Mom."

It's 3 p.m., and the mail is delivered. I can't wait; I drop everything in my hands and run to the mailbox. Immediately I recognize it. I stop breathing and slow down. Slowly, step-by-step I walk closer to what I can't accept. My first package has been returned, and knowing that it will take another six-eight weeks before he'll get it, I scream in frustration, and then I cry. The package is damaged as if it has been in the war itself. I open it, and I unload all the goodies. The homemade cookies are crushed, and I'll have to throw them away. I dry my eyes several times when unpacking each and every item, transferring it to a new box. I leave my son a new letter, telling him that it wasn't my fault.

Days go by, weeks go by, even some months. The war has been declared over, but it's not. My son is still not back home. I continue to carry packages to the post office; I have stopped counting the number of boxes I have packed. The post office is busy, people buying stamps, picking up their mail, returning too small panties from Victoria's Secret, or some other inferior activities. "Have they all forgotten," I ask myself? Nobody seems to notice my box or me; nobody feels my need to tell about my brave son and his comrades. Nobody knows that just the other day I found a photo of my son in the newspaper, a photo of my son carrying a wounded comrade. They have no idea how I felt, when I was staring at the cruel proof that my son is still at war. We forget so quickly and move on. Perhaps that's what keeps us alive.... I don't know.

The postal worker looks up and smiles at me. "When will he be back?"

"Another seven months," I answer, and I'm again reminded of our long separation.

I thought I knew...so how could I be so mistaken?

"You told me when you left that you hated war, but you told me too, that you hated the idea of genocide even more. Gosh, I miss you so!"

One true moment of many different true moments. Maripaz Garcia's boyfriend, Enrique, getting flowers from Iraqi children.

Renate “Rain” Nietzold’s son, Shawn, with a MK 19-3, 40 mm grenade machine gun, Iraq, 2003. “He was on a convoy and the truck in front of him got hit with a missile. His friend lost a leg.”

Family and friends of the 4th ID anxiously waiting the last hour before their loved ones are expected to show up in the gym at Fort Hood, Texas, March 2004. “I am looking forward to their homecoming, and I cannot wait to have my husband safe at home once again.”

A Soldier's Christmas Letter to His Mother

By Valerie Pugh

Valerie Pugh's son, Specialist Armando Rodriguez, is a medic with the 1-67 Armor, Alpha Company, 4th Infantry Division, from Fort Hood, Texas. He is in Iraq, just north of Baghdad. Valerie Pugh lives in El Paso, Texas, where she works as the administrative assistant for the Regional Vice President of Texas Gas Service Company. She and her husband of 20 years, Ron, have two sons, Mando and Justin.

During my son's deployment, there was a constant stream of uplifting letters and encouraging words going to him, to help him through bleak, dangerous days in Iraq. Imagine my surprise when I received the following letter from him. In the midst of all he was going through, he was encouraging me!

4 December 2003
Dear Mom,

I don't really know how to start this letter. Instead of having to write this, I wish I could be there to give you a hug. I often imagine you giving me a hug out here; it gets me through the long days. I love your hugs. And then your great smell. That particular smell that reminds me of 'mom'. I miss your hugs sooo much. I just want you to know how much you mean to me. You've had nothing but faith in me all through the years, supporting me in no matter what I do. No matter what crazy idea comes to mind, you never shun it away. There's been so many times that most parents would have given up and gotten tired, but you never did. You always tried to teach and show me the right things. All the times you've told me how I was your everything. Truth is the exact opposite, you're MY everything! There is no possible way I could describe in words how much you mean to me.

Your perseverance in life has been inspirational to me. Just know that I'm going to be all right. This Christmas is going to be hard on us both, but like you said, before we know it, I'll be home and we'll be talking all day and night. It sometimes amazes me the relationship we have. Sometimes I wish others had the same, so they could see what it feels like to have such a wonderful relationship with their mom.

Before I close, I just want you to know that you have NOTHING to worry about. I'll be okay. I love you so much, mom. I couldn't ask for anything more in a mother. Thank you for being there for me. There's nothing I wouldn't do for you. Hope to see you very soon.

I love you! Always and forever,
Your son,
Armando

"Before he would leave, he would always make sure to kiss my forehead and tell me that he loved me, and that he would be back on Sunday. I thought that would be all Devin would have to do. I never dreamed of him leaving me behind and going off to war."

A Grandmother

By Margee Willy

Margee Willy's 20-year-old grandson, Dustin, is deployed to Iraq. Private First Class "Dus" Patterson, is a tank driver with HHC, 1st Battalion, 67 Armor. He went into Iraq, April 8, 2003. Margee Willy runs a bed and breakfast in a small town just outside Rapid City, South Dakota, called Wasta.

In September 2002, my 20-year-old grandson was a new recruit at Fort Knox, Kentucky. We had been hearing stirrings of an ominous nature emanating from Iraq. This boy had looked carefully at his career choices before ultimately deciding on the Army. On my trip to Fort Knox, seeing my grandson in uniform, tall, standing straight and proud, and so handsome was as emotionally overwhelming as the first day I saw him two hours old! I was prepared to be overwhelmed at the first sight, not the second!

After completing training and waiting to report to Fort Hood, we were able to have some time together here in South Dakota. The days passed too quickly and departure day was upon us. His uniform needed pressing and I insisted on the privilege of doing the job. As I smoothed the trousers and straightened the creases, I looked at my hands, and knew I had joined an elite sisterhood going back through the ages. How many mothers and grandmothers have smoothed and pressed these garments of brotherhood of service? How many have known the swelling of pride in this honorable young man doing his duty? How many have known the corresponding welling of abject fear at the thought of sending this child of their soul into known harms way, down a path of experiences that will forever alter all he is? This would be how my grandmother felt when her grandson, child of her soul, sailed away to the Pacific.

Grandmothers whose loss was in the war to make this country free, grandmothers whose loss came in the war that divided this country. A grandmother who has waited for some good news from

Korea, so her personal shining star could come home to Tennessee, where, after all, he belonged. Grandmothers, through time, who knew the most precious gift they could give their country, is this proud honorable young man who will do his duty for his country. This grandmother's job description is pretty narrow. I write letters and send stuff. I support his mom and communicate with his girlfriend, and continue to feel the same pride and love I've always felt, and now add an extra measure of respect.

When he was a little guy, he would call and say, "Okay Marg, I can come out for a few days. Meet us in the canyon to pick me up."

Checking the atlas, it's not so far. "Okay Dus, I can come for a few days, meet me in London!" I could do that—no problem!

In my mind, I sit by and hold the hand of this boy's mother. We've shared a lot: sometimes I've given strength, and sometimes I've taken strength. We have been outrageously silly, gaining release in laughter. We have cried, and our mingled tears speak of fear, loneliness and disappointment. I hold this woman in respect, admiration and love. We two know of the great love each has for this boy, this boy who is now a man. I think no one else in the world knows, but she understands how I feel. How glad I am to have her.

"My thoughts and prayers are with all our soldiers and their families, my prayer is that they all return home safe to their loved ones who are so very proud of them. They are all our Heroes!"

Wives

Rachel E. Lies

Lauren King

Kristy Baron

Guita M. Leeds

Margaret Hodges

Sherri Martin and Kids

Wives

What it Means to Love a Soldier

By Jamie Reese, Special to American Forces Press Service

FORT HOOD, Texas, Oct. 8, 2003—She stands in line at the post office waiting to send a package to her husband, a U.S. Army soldier serving in Kuwait. Envelopes, pens, paper, stamps, sunscreen, eye-drops, gum, batteries, powdered Gatorade, baby wipes and Twizzlers.

He said he needed the sunscreen and baby wipes. She threw in the Twizzlers.

There's a common bond at the post office in this military town. People aren't just sending letters and packages; they are sending smiles, hope, love and just a touch of home. People look around at the others, sharing their concern, fear and pride. They take comfort knowing they are not alone.

—Courtesy American Forces Press Service

A Soldier's Wife

By Marsha Bourquin

Marsha Bourquin's husband is with Headquarters and Headquarters Company, 2/8 Infantry (Mechanized), 4th Infantry Division (ID) and was deployed to Iraq, March 2003.

She resides in Itasca, Texas, with her mother, Pat, and her nineteen-year-old daughter, Teri, while her husband, Troy, is deployed. She works as a Public Safety Communicator for the Hillsboro Police Department.

My life as the wife of a deployed Soldier began March 27, 2003, as my husband, Specialist Troy Bourquin, headed to Iraq in support of "Operation Iraqi Freedom."

The first few weeks following his deployment were quite an adjustment period for me. Days were suddenly spent waiting for the mail, and awaiting word that his unit made it safely to their destination in Iraq, where his tour of duty would start. Then, the really hard part began. As attacks on our troops escalated, the anxiety set in, as I found myself waiting, worrying, and jumping every time the telephone rang. Communication was still not very good at this time, which only increased my anxiety about his safety. I tried to keep myself as busy as possible; I began to keep a scrapbook for "Operation Iraqi Freedom." I also began to create a keepsake book for all his letters.

Then I began to search for information—as much as I could—about his unit and Iraq. That was when I discovered and began to receive the 4th ID Daily Update from Iraq, which has been a great help for me ever since. It makes such a difference to learn that other families are going through the exact same things that I am experiencing these days. In July, things got even harder when we received word that our soldiers' deployment would last for a year. This was a bitter pill to swallow!

After spending two days crying, I realized that it was my job to do my very best to support my husband and keep up his morale. I needed to be strong for him, as his country needed him to fulfill a duty. I continued to write letters to him every day, and send care packages out every week, but I have to confess that some days I just felt overwhelmed. Lonely and worried for my husband's safety, it was so easy to become depressed. Just when I thought I couldn't take it anymore, God was there, and my prayers were answered. A phone call in the middle of the night. A ten-minute call worked a miracle for morale on both ends. Just hearing his voice telling me that he was all right lifted my spirits and gave me the much-needed strength to stay strong and remain a good support system for my husband.

The most difficult time for me was yet to come. September 30th was our wedding anniversary. We had never been apart on our anniversary, but my sister managed to push me out of the house by inviting me to dinner and a movie. My husband was able to call me the day before our anniversary and send a card via e-mail, too. It was not the kind of anniversary I had imagined, but it is only one out of many in the years to come when we again will be able to celebrate together.

Then one day I heard the best words ever: "Mid-Tour Leave." I was on an emotional roller coaster at this time, but the initial excitement suddenly turned to worry. Would he be eligible for leave? And if he was eligible, could I then face putting him back on that plane for a second time? Because I knew it would be harder the second time around.

My husband came home on leave November 3, 2003. The night before he was due to arrive, my sister said I was like a kid on Christmas Eve, too excited to eat or sleep. His 15-day leave was a wonderful time for our family and us. I was really concerned he might return home a different person, and even though he had seen some terrible things, he was still the same loving, caring man I married eight years ago. I did not push him on his feelings about Iraq, or on what he has witnessed, I just let him set the tone. He did tell me some disturbing things, but I just listened as he told me the sad story about having to work on a friend of his (he is a Medic) who had been badly injured. I listened, swelling with pride as he told me how he had earned his Combat Medic Badge. These heart-to-heart talks we shared are very near and dear to me and only made our time together more precious.

My husband left again for Iraq, November 26, 2003, and, as I had feared, it was very hard to watch him walk away for the second time. It was just as hard for him to take that walk, but he believes in what he is doing and feels very honored to serve his country.

I am now back being the "wife of a deployed soldier." I mark off the days on my calendar until his return in April. He made it safely back to his unit at Camp Normandy. They now have a phone center and he has been able to call home almost every day. This is a great comfort for us both—to be able hear each other's voice on a regular basis.

I know there will be difficult days ahead. Every day I run into at least one person who asks about my husband, and tells me how grateful they are for his service, but unless you have a loved one who is over in a distant land, you can never really understand what the family left behind is going through. I have learned a lot over these past months from doing minor repairs around the house to learning how to fill my time and cope with the stress of everyday life without my husband at home. I am very blessed for the support I have received from my family and friends. My sister Kim has been my rock and is there for me day and night. I would never have been able to make it without her love and understanding.

My co-workers at the Hillsboro Police Department have been great. They ask me on a daily basis about my husband, and if I am doing okay. They really went the extra mile while he was home on leave rearranging their shifts so that I could be off work the entire 15 days. For this, I will be eternally grateful.

My goal for the remaining months of my husband's tour is to remain strong and loyal to him and to support him as he performs his duty so far away from his country and his family. My thoughts and prayers are with all our soldiers and their families, my prayer is that they all return home safe to their loved ones who are so very proud of them. They are all our Heroes!

A Spouse and a Veteran

By Guita Leeds

Guita Leeds is the spouse of an U.S. Army Officer in Iraq, but she is also a veteran of the Army. She served for seven years in both the Chemical Corps and as a tank turret mechanic. Guita Leeds, a stay-at-home mom for two boys, is originally from Illinois, but currently stationed at Fort Hood, TX. Her husband was deployed to Iraq as the Battalion Chemical Officer for 3-16th Field Artillery in April 2003.

I write this not only as the spouse of an Army Officer in Iraq, but as a veteran of the Army myself. I served for seven years in both the Chemical Corps and as a tank turret mechanic. Therefore, I know the military from both sides, and in times of peace and war. Thankfully, my time was served during peace, not war. Now I am dealing with wartime as the wife of a soldier.

The past eight months have been the hardest I've had to deal with in my 43 years. I've become sole provider for the family, while my husband is off protecting our way of life and also making a better life for the people of Iraq. I do my best to keep a smile on my face, so as not to let my children see the pain I deal with each day. Some days it is easier than others, but I manage as best I can. I want them to be children as long as possible, and not have this time be too hard on them. They, too, miss their father, as I do, and long for his safe return home to us.

The phone calls are few at times, but the letters keep coming. They've recently acquired Internet access, and it is good to be able to chat with him in real time. His letters sometimes tell of the tense times he is going through, but he tries not to worry me with all of that. I can usually read between the lines, and credit him for thinking of my peace of mind in such a difficult time and place. Not only is he a world away from the ones he loves, but he is also in harm's way on a daily basis.

Although my time in the service was served during peacetime,

I know what its like to be away from the ones you love, to be far away in a foreign country, not knowing the language. You serve your country, not only for your family, but for those you have never met. You worry and wonder if those you have left behind are doing well. You want to be there for them, but have chosen a way of life that not all agree with. You give of yourself on a daily basis so others can have the freedoms that many take for granted.

I am proud to have given seven years of my life for my country, and even prouder yet of my husband for making the sacrifice he is making now. He was not drafted into the Army like in times gone by. He chose to give of himself for both his family and his country. He proudly wears the uniform of an Officer in the US Army, and for this I am grateful.

I know deep down that there is always the possibility he could be wounded, or worse yet, killed, while over there. I try not to let this rule my days, but I do not kid myself either. Each night before I go to sleep, I hug the bear he sent me, and wish for his swift and safe return. I hold tight to that bear as I sleep, and send positive thoughts out to him. I will keep the home fires burning until he returns.

I know when my husband returns, there will be much he has been through and seen that he will not wish to talk about. I will be there for him, as I always am, to help him over the rough spots. We have both sacrificed much in the past eight months and I feel it will only serve to make us both stronger people. Hopefully in the future, we will look back on this time in our lives and be thankful we made it through all of it.

For those who have never been a part of the military, I ask only one thing: take the time out to thank those who serve, and have served, for giving you the freedoms you have each day. For without these people, you would not be where you are today. I am proud to be a veteran, a mother, and the spouse of a military man!

"It seems that so many have already forgotten that our soldiers are still dying, and getting hurt every day. I miss my son so much! I often feel that our soldiers have been put on the back burner, that our brave soldiers are not getting the praise they so rightly deserve."

Sergeant Jacobe Kiser in Iraq, 2003.
"We have that picture of you on the computer... there is that Brad Pitt smile."

Photo to Daddy in Iraq. Sherri Martin's 2-year old daughter Julie, and 5-month old son Josh, who was born while her husband was in Iraq.

US soldiers playing spades.
"Hopefully in the future, we will look back on this time in our lives and be thankful we made it through all of it."

How I Feel

By Kristy Baron

Kristy Baron's husband, Staff Sergeant Joseph Baron, has been in the Army for 13 years and was deployed to Iraq, March 2, 2003. She gave birth to their son Hunter, on April 24, 2003. Kristy Baron lives in Cumberland City, Tennessee. She is employed with BellSouth Telecommunications.

My name is Kristy Baron and I live in Tennessee, near fort Campbell. My husband, Staff Sergeant Joseph Baron, left for Iraq on March 2, 2003. When he left, I was 8-1/2 months pregnant with our first child. This is our first time apart since we were married and it has been so hard with him being gone.

Our son was born on April 24, 2003, but he became ill and stopped breathing. He had to be put on life support, so he was transported to Vanderbilt University Medical Center where he remained in NICU for five days. I was devastated because I had delivered him by Cesarean section and couldn't leave the hospital. I am very thankful that I live near my parents and they were able to go be with our baby while I couldn't. I felt so bad because for the first few days of my son's life, he didn't have either of his parents with him. I was really upset with the Army! Our son was on life support, and yet they wouldn't let my husband come home. I am so thankful to God that our baby, Hunter, is okay now. It ended up that he had swallowed some amniotic fluid and because he was born by Cesarean section, it got into his lungs and caused him to stop breathing. He is a perfectly healthy, happy six-month-old little boy now.

My husband is still in Iraq, and still hasn't met Hunter. It is heartbreaking that he will miss all of these months with him. I am so happy when Hunter does something new, but I still feel a little sad that his daddy can't be here to witness it. I never realized how hard it was to be an Army wife until I got the word that my husband would be going to Iraq. I have learned that an Army wife has to be able to do everything on her own, plus be both Mommy and Daddy.

When the news came that he would be there for a full year, I just sat down and cried. I am so anxious for him to meet little Hunter and to see the new house that I have bought for us and moved us to since he left. I want him to meet our new puppy; I want to be able to carry on a conversation with him without the line getting disconnected or having a bad connection. It seems as if I am constantly praying for his safety these days, with all of the attacks still happening, I am terrified that something will happen to him. He sometimes tells me stories that scare me even more, but I know that he needs someone to talk to, and I can almost be certain that he doesn't let me know a lot of what his daily life is like in Iraq, because he doesn't want me to worry.

My husband has been in the Army for 13 years and has recently submitted his paperwork to get out. His fear is that he would be away more than half of the time until he retires if he doesn't get out. He received a Bronze Star for leadership and bravery, and I thought that would change his mind, but it didn't. I am so proud of my husband for all that he has accomplished in Iraq and in his military career, but I almost feel a sense of relief that he will not have to go back to Iraq or any other war zone, and that he will be home with me.

"Being in Iraq in July is not something that is easily replicated in the United States. The only place with comparable heat and dust conditions is Death Valley, California. The average daily temperature was 125 degrees Fahrenheit. The Schmal winds occurred daily—30-50 knot winds that would just blow dust everywhere, including into every little pore of your skin."

4th ID soldier killed in Iraq

By Steven R. Hurst
The Associated Press From Killeen Daily Hearld, Sunday, Aug. 3

BAGHDAD, Iraq—A 4th Infantry Division soldier was killed and three were wounded Friday in a rocket-propelled grenade attack on their convoy east of Baghdad, military officials said Saturday. Also Saturday, Saddam Hussein's two elder sons and a grandson were buried as martyrs in rocky soil near the deposed leader's hometown, where insurgents afterward attacked U.S. troops with three remote controlled bombs.

Almost a Soldier

By Lee Woodruff

Lee Woodruff's husband, Bob, a reporter for ABC News, was one of the many embedded journalists in Iraq. He was with the First Marine Division during the Iraq war, from January to April 2003. Lee Woodruff lives in Rye, New York, with her husband and four children. She is a part-time writer and marketing consultant.

Two hours after the September 11th attacks, my husband, then a London-based television journalist, boarded a plane for Afghanistan. There was no time for him to say goodbye to my older children, Mack; then ten, and Cathryn, eight—finishing their day at The American School. Our 18-month-old twins merrily waved "bye bye" to Daddy, oblivious to the fact that he would be missing the ritual of books and snuggles that evening. Unaware of the news shocking the world, I would have missed him myself had I dawdled any longer at the grocery store.

I arrived at our house only to find Bob on the front stoop, hastily-packed duffelbag weighing down one shoulder. It was our anniversary that night, but the celebration would obviously have to wait. Days dragged into weeks and weeks into months. During that next year, he was gone far more than he was home, often leaving for six-week stretches.

That first day, watching the surreal images of the twin towers on television, I vowed to keep our family life as normal as possible, despite his absence. On some levels, that was surprisingly easy, given our hectic schedules, soccer games, spelling tests, birthday parties and Halloween costumes. Like the military, I decided that a kind of "don't ask, don't tell" policy would be best for all of us. If the kids didn't witness my fears, then they would take my lead and feel safe themselves.

With cable access to American news shows, I taped Bob's pieces at night to watch his reports in the morning. I felt certain that the image of their father on the screen, and the familiar sound of his voice, would reassure them he was all right, despite what the pictures were showing. I couldn't have been more wrong. As the fury escalated, the story involved an angry anti-American mob and in another instance, the Taliban chased Bob's convoy through the desert. Although I began heavily censoring what I showed them, my son Mack developed serious problems falling asleep. When he learned at school that four journalists had been killed, his sleep issues, not surprisingly, worsened.

One night, I decided to say a prayer with Mack for Dad's safety. Somewhere in my words and exhausted bare emotion, he sensed something new. It was fear. "I thought I was the only one who was scared," Mack whispered, his confession obviously filling him with relief and release. Through his tears and his bear hug that night, I learned an important lesson. By trying to make our lives seem normal, I had left my children to carry their fears all alone.

This year, based back in New York, Bob is one of the many embedded journalists in Iraq. As I write, he is crawling across the desert in a long line of tanks; eating, and sleeping, and surviving sandstorms with his military division. While he reports on the unfolding war abroad, parents all over the world are trying, once again, to create a veneer of normalcy for their children, while weighing the potential risks and dangers of flooding them with too much information.

Unlike military spouses, I can communicate somewhat regularly with Bob by phone. Yet the isolation I feel in my suburban New York community, makes me long for what I imagine to be the collective wisdom of a military base—support groups for spouses, parenting classes on how to deal with stress and anxiety. Instead, I am here on a leafy street 'embedded' among civilian families. My friends and acquaintances try desperately to be supportive. They flatter me endlessly with compliments about how well I am managing on my own with four children. There are days I believe what they say, that maybe I am made of stronger stuff. But those days are rare. Usually, I just feel as anyone would in my position—tired, frightened, worried, and sometimes resentful of Bob's career.

I am not different, and I don't want to be set apart as superhuman. Really, all I want is to belong at a time when feeling 'normal' is an ultimate goal.

Recently, during a conference, my daughter's fourth grade teacher told me that Cathryn had confided to him numerous times how fearful she was for her father's safety. Immediately I felt that I had failed as a parent. Was I not giving my children sufficient outlet for their worries? Should we be discussing the war more at home? When Bob was first sent to Kuwait, Cathryn had been inconsolable over her father's absence at night. Nothing I could say or do eased her concern. Exasperated, I found myself wanting to scream at her, "Don't you think I miss him too?"

Yet I found the strength to hold back my own tears for fear of terrifying my young daughter. Knowing I was concerned about Bob was one thing. Seeing me collapse into an emotional heap was another. Then Cathryn's teacher turned to me and asked quite pointedly, "How are you doing?"

Tears filled my eyes over his unexpected, kind question. "I don't know how to parent in this situation," I confided. "There are no rule books for this kind of thing, and I just want to get it right for my children."

"Just keep doing what you are doing," he assured me. "You've given her the tools to tackle all of these complicated emotions, and she reached out to me too."

What I rediscovered, with the help of her teacher, is that we all need other outlets. A mother can't be everything to her children, nor should she be. And just as they needed to open up to others, so did I. Trying to be brave was killing me.

On the night that the war began, I boarded a plane to London with my two older children, leaving my twin three-year-olds behind with Bob's parents. They, too, needed a distraction, and chasing after two active three-year-olds would certainly provide one. The trip back to London had been booked since August. Well-meaning friends had tried to talk me out of going, and I had to weigh the emotional cost of canceling our trip. The children had been looking forward to visiting for months, and were surprisingly oblivious to the fact that many considered it dangerous to travel at this time. To cancel now, I decided, would send a message of terror greater than what they were already processing. We would go.

While flying over the Atlantic, the pilot's calm, clipped British accent announced that the bombing campaign with Iraq had commenced. A sick feeling hit my stomach like a punch, as we hurtled through the air, hanging above the time zones. Somewhere down there, my husband was moving under cover of night. He had told me that once the war began, a 'black out' period would ensue. He would be out of communication for days.

Being in London that first weekend of the war took our minds temporarily off world events. The children enjoyed seeing old friends, and I had a break from my routine. We all purposely avoided watching the news. When we touched back down in New York, I breathed a heavy sigh of relief. My decision had not been wrong.

Now, like so many others, I sit glued to the TV. The images are hard for me to watch, and yet I can't seem to tear myself away. Occasionally, I let the children see one of Bob's reports. Mack finds it "cool" when he spots his Dad riding on a tank. He believes that the military will protect his father. I let him hold onto that at all costs.

When Bob and I talk on the choppy satellite phone, it's easy to hide my cracking voice from him. My concerns about bills, taxes, and doctor's appointments are so far from his world right now. I can visualize the grueling conditions under which he is working and practically smell the sweat, tension and sand through the receiver. While I need to be strong for him on the phone, I now open up to my friends in private.

And each night when I tuck four pairs of anxious eyes into bed, I no longer work so hard to hide the occasional tear. Instead, we talk about Daddy; how much we miss him, how strong and brave he is, and how concerned we are for his safety. And if we all have a little cry together, that's okay too. Our reality is that Daddy is in the center of a war zone right now. And the most normal thing is for us to feel worried.

How Does it Feel to be A Soldiers's Wife?

By Jessica Howard

Jessica Howard is a wife of a soldier with the 4th Infantry Division. Her husband joined the Army two weeks before he turned 35, and was deployed shortly afterward. Jessica Howard's husband, Gary, is currently serving in Iraq with the 1-10 Cavalry, 4th Infantry Division. They have been married for almost seven years and have two children: Skylar, eight, and Gary, six. They currently reside in Harker Heights, Texas, but are from Middletown, New York.

It was a hot July summer night in Virginia Beach. My husband and I were sitting outside talking to our neighbors, when out of the blue, he said to me, " I should join the Army."

I looked puzzled and asked why. He was upset because he had no future in his current job, no financial security, and no retirement. I replied joking around, "You're too old to join."

The next morning when I woke up, he told me that he had an appointment with a recruiter for the Army. The cutoff age was 35, which meant he had just about two weeks to join. We went to the recruiter together, and she was so good. She explained everything to us. My husband wanted to join. So he did.

Just one week later, his recruiter came to the house picked him up and drove him to Richmond, Virginia. I remember it so well. My husband looked at me and said, "Don't worry, I will be home in December of this year."

The kids were outside crying and hugging daddy, and so was I. The months seemed to pass by so slowly, although I got to talk to him more than I had expected to. He was Platoon Leader in his unit, and all the drill sergeants loved him.

December finally came. My sister-in-law, my two nieces, my son, my daughter, and I hopped into the minivan and headed for Fort Leonard Wood, Missouri. I was so excited. The last time I had seen him was July 31. I remember how proud I was of him, and I was so excited to watch him graduate. Well, wouldn't you know...

we went to the wrong graduation! We were at the Military Police graduation, realizing it after I finally read the sign. I turned and asked a military person next to me, "Where is the chemical graduation?"

He told me that it was down the road. So needless to say, we ran and finally got to see the last five minutes of my husband's graduation ceremony. He came home with us after the ceremony, but had to return January 3, 2003 for "Lima-5" classes. That meant another six weeks without my husband. "That's ok," I thought. "After this, it will all be over and we will move to his first duty station."

The day came when he called and said we were moving to Fort Hood, Texas. "Ok," I thought. "Texas is fine."

He arrived at Fort Hood, February 15, 2003. A week later he called and informed me he couldn't come get me because he was heading off to Iraq soon.

I was lucky enough to see him for three wonderful days before he went to Iraq. His lieutenant flew him home, and then he drove one of our cars back to Texas. I was completely alone now. He would be 8,000 miles away from me. Three weeks since July of 2002 was all I got to spend with my husband. He called me from time to time, and was so worried that the kids would forget him, and that I would move on and find someone new. To set his mind at ease, I decided to leave everything I knew behind and move to Texas to wait for his return. I figured he would be gone until Thanksgiving, but it turns out he won't be back home before April 2004. So, I put on my brave face for my kids, and started a journey that seems impossible to me.

Basically, I am a single mom raising two kids. I am now dealing with my son who's having a real hard time with daddy being gone. You meet people from his unit that you would like to call friends, but in reality they are not. I am a lot older than most of these girls.

The letters come every day from him. The phone calls, well, they are so few and far between. It hurts more to hear his voice, anyway. I stand in line at the post office to mail packages to him. That seems to make him happy, a little piece of home for him.

Iraq Remains Dangerous for U.S. Troops; Security Operations Continue

By Gerry J. Gilmore, American Forces Press Service

WASHINGTON, May 27, 2003—Several U.S. troops were killed by hostile action or accidents in Iraq over the past few days as U.S., coalition and Iraqi operations to enhance law and order in that Middle East country continued.

Two U.S. Army soldiers were killed and nine injured during a May 27 firefight with hostile forces near Fallujah, according to a U.S. Central Command press release. The release noted the aggressors attacked the American troops with rocket-propelled grenades and small-arms fire from a mosque, which is a violation of the law of war.

The U.S. soldiers' response killed two enemy troops, according to the release, while six were captured.

—Courtesy American Forces Press Service

The Long Road Home

By Sophia Garcia

Sophia Garcia's husband, who is with the Army's 4th Infantry Division, has been in the military for four years and was deployed to Iraq. Sophia Garcia lives in a big military community in Copperas Cove, Texas. Sophia married Specialist Gersain Garcia on Feb. 7, 2003 when they realized he was being deployed to Iraq.

My husband, Specialist Garcia Gersain, is serving with the US Army's 4th Infantry Division. My husband is in the Infantry. We live in Copperas Cove, Texas, a big military community. My husband has been in the military for four years. Two of those, he was stationed in Italy. He hopes to take our daughter and me there some day soon. We got married February 7, 2003. We married, since I was one month pregnant, and because we had been told Garcia was to be deployed to Iraq sometime soon. We really needed the medical benefits, too. Otherwise, we would have waited awhile before we tied the knot.

I am very proud of my husband; he is very strong, physically and mentally. Garcia is very driven, and loves his job in the Army. The day he came home with the news that they were going to be deployed to Iraq, I was so sad. I thought about how I was going to go through this pregnancy alone. There was a probability that he wouldn't be able to come home for the birth, and both of our families live in California. My family could not afford to come out here to stay with me, and neither could Garcia's family. My husband and I were very stressed about what I was going to do.

From about the beginning of January 2003, Garcia and his comrades' work schedule intensified. To make it to work on time, he would get up at 4:45 in the morning and not return home before 9:00 or 10:00 at night, just to eat, and then go to sleep. There was not really any time to spend together before he left.

From then on, he would often come home and say, "Okay, we're leaving in three days."

Then those three days would come and go, and nothing happened. Each and every time I would try to prepare myself to say goodbye, and then again, the date got pushed back. This went on until they left, April 2nd.

The day they left stands out as the most emotional and difficult day of my life. That early morning they still had to go to work, but they got to come home for half a day. They all had to be back around 5:00 the same evening, so we didn't even get to spend much time that day either. We, the families, were told that we would get an hour to say goodbye, but they cut it down to half an hour. I was really angry. I tried not to cry because Garcia dislikes seeing me crying. The instant he started to put his gear on it hit me… he was actually leaving. My husband was actually going to war, and there was a risk that he might not return. There was a risk that he would never meet our beautiful baby. I guess he couldn't stand to see me cry, so he told me I had to leave, and then pushed me away. I was upset about that, but I knew, too, that it would be very difficult for him to express his sadness.

When I retuned home alone that evening, everything reminded me of him. I was constantly crying and glued to the news. Now, I guess, I am kind of numb to the situation. I have to be strong for us, and for our little girl, who was born September 14, 2003. She is the reason for me to keep going, knowing that I can't break down, our little girl needs me as much as I need her and her dad.

This experience has actually brought my husband and me much closer. We talk about the fun stuff on the phone, so he gets distracted from everything over there. I try to make him laugh because not too many people can make him laugh. He tells me that when he's talking to me, that is when he de-stresses. I am looking forward to their homecoming, and I cannot wait to have my husband safe at home once again.

"Touch someone's life and remember that they may be saving yours."

Enduring Fear

By Rachel E. Lies

Rachel E. Lies and her husband, Matt, are both active duty Air Force members. Matt, and her brother, a U.S. Marine, were both deployed during "Operation Iraqi Freedom. She joined the United States Air Force in April 2001. Rachel E Lies is originally from Ohio, but is currently stationed in Florida. Her husband, Matt, is also in the USAF and her brother, Craig, is in the United States Marine Corps."

The day I realized my life was turning upside down was September 11, 2001. Five-and-a-half months after raising my right hand, swearing to defend the United States, I watched the World Trade Center fall, like a child's play blocks. When I entered the Air Force, not too much was happening in the world. The Gulf War was over, and the conflicts in Kosovo and Bosnia were dimming. But on this day, I watched the scrambling begin and realized the horror of what was happening.

After that day, America was not the same, and, neither was I. There was always a constant fear lying deep in myself of what could happen if we went to war. As events escalated and hostility grew, leading to the war in 2003, I married an active duty Air Force member, Matt. It was real love, and has only grown since. It is hard, both of us donning the uniform everyday, but we manage by keeping close and holding our feet down. On January 28, 2003, four days after I turned twenty-one years old, President Bush gave his State of the Union address. My mom called from Ohio since we are stationed in Florida, telling me to turn the TV on, and to call her back when it was over. I ran to the back of our cramped apartment, yelling for Matt to leave the computer alone for a few minutes. I received some grumbles in return after yelling that this was important. "This is our Commander in Chief!" Finally, he came out and sat on the other end of the couch, since we were both agitated.

Hearing President Bush proclaim that America was going to

invade Iraq, I felt my heart jump, as if I entered a dream. *Us*? *Going to war*? Trying to get a grip, I called my crying mother as Matt wandered back to the computer, trying to go unnoticed. That was when the terrifying, agonizing worrying began for my mother. You see, I was not the only military member in my family. My younger brother, Craig, had joined the Marine Corps the year before. It was a gutsy move for my brother to claim his independence and show that he was different than me.

Not long after the State of the Union address, my brother received orders to the Middle East. My mother was frantic. Our family had never been around military people, and we did not know what lives of soldiers were like. Craig could not calm her nerves, as his were rattling, too. So, I took what I knew, which was not much, and tried to calm her down. She was wondering, crying, and hoping maybe, he would not go.

My parents were not the only ones worried; I was too. How could my little brother go? Granted he had chosen the life of a Marine, but I still felt compelled to protect him, just as we had helped each other growing up. *He can't go without me*! *I have to go, too, I can't leave him*! It was hard and nerve-racking knowing I could not do anything, and that he was grown up now. My little brother, my hero and person I most wanted to be like, was going to the desert.

Soon after he left, I departed for Oklahoma, for a training class. My class was in the evenings, so I had all day to watch CNN and tell my mom what I thought, when she asked questions: "He's okay! No, he's not even near there. Why would he be on a helicopter? He's supply; he would only go the front lines in an extreme situation. The bombs won't hit them!"

Time flew, letters came and went. Phones were ringing with the latest news of a letter or even a phone call from Craig. When he finally came home, my parents and sister-in-law, Amanda, were beside themselves with excitement. Until I gave my mom the bad news. Matt had gotten orders for the desert.

This can't be happening, I thought. Craig just got back. I don't want to worry anymore. Soon after, Matt left.

At the airport I kept my composure as best as I could. I didn't want him upset, and this dream seemed surreal. Once I walked out of the airport, my composure left with his plane into the sky, and I cried. I cried, and I was angry. Angry because two people I loved dearly were away from my grasp, and I could not keep them safe.

I don't remember much of his absence from me. He was gone for only three months, but each day seemed like an eternity in itself. People around me were not much help. Always wondering how he was doing and where he was. It helped to talk about him, but it was I who needed human contact, and a shoulder to cry on, that I never found.

Three months after Matt's return, we attended our squadron's Christmas party. Since we would not be able to see family this year during the holidays, I was having fun, enjoying the company. After socializing for a bit, the speaker, Technical Sergeant Williams, began speaking in a somber tone.

"From the shot heard round the world ... to the war on terrorism and Operation Iraqi Freedom, and Enduring Freedom, our nation's military personnel and their families have made many sacrifices and faced many hardships to ensure that our great nation remained free. At this time, we would like to take the opportunity to recognize a few special people in attendance tonight. As I call your name, I ask that you and your spouse, or guest, please join the commander and his lovely bride on the stage."

Matt and I were the second or third couple called up to the stage, and we slowly made our way to the front. I didn't know what to expect, since there was no warning. We waited and gazed out into the crowd, as the rest of the couples made their way to the stage.

"The sacrifices and hardships you faced and endured while being separated from your loved ones, whether only by miles within the United States, or by the oceans and deserts to the Middle East, are a testament to what it takes to support the Air Force when duty calls. The airman endures the hazards and dangers of the deployment, while the family members left on the home front are thrust into the trials of keeping daily life running smoothly."

"Tonight we present to you a 2003 holiday tree ornament as a small token of our appreciation for the sacrifices and hardships each of you faced during your deployments. When you place it on your tree this year, and for years to come, we hope it reminds you of the strength that lives within your family. Together, you can overcome all challenges. Thank you for your service to our great nation."

Our commander, Lieutenant Colonel Eckert, gave Matt the beautiful ornament, while Mrs. Eckert presented me with a red rose and a big hug. It took everything in my soul to hold back the sobbing in my heart. Suddenly I felt overwhelmed by all the memories of Matt not being here and what we both had to endure: the feelings of emptiness, tears on my pillow, and hearing the disappointment in his voice on the answering machine when he called, and I wasn't home.

I still think of the time without him now and again. I would have completely broken down without him, had it not been for angels in my life. My parents, who always called, cried with me, and gave me support I cannot begin to describe, as it was immense. God and his angels were always with me, wiping away my tears and giving me hope. With all of this "human" support, my three kitties were always there. Happy, sweet faces and loving tenderness was always there, instead of an empty, cold house. Their loud purrs and endless cuddling helped me when I cried. I was beside myself when my littlest one, lying next to me while I was sobbing, tenderly put his little paw on my eye, as if telling me it was going to be okay. They are my little angels from God and I'm so thankful they are with me.

My heart ached and always will for the families of the fallen, and soldiers that have been away from their families for months and maybe years now. The wives and mothers left behind are people who can hold their ground in the face of fear and loneliness. They are heroes among us who are sometimes forgotten. I applaud them, and I am grateful I can hold my head high among them.

Bee Pedersen's son, Kevin, in a guard tower. Saddam Hussein's birthday palace, Tikrit, Iraq.
"My baby, 19-years old, is going to war. I cry inside... why, why, why?"

"It hurts me deeply to hear that Tom has lost his friend. It is so hard to deal with when you hear that another soldier has passed away. I believe that I'm starting to feel and think like everybody else around me. 'Why are we over there? Where are the WMD's? Where is Saddam?' It's so wrong for us being there. More and more soldiers are losing their lives trying to help these people regain freedom and do they want it...? I would say to Bush if I saw him right now, 'Bring our soldiers home!'"

Secrets From Within

By Michell Gonzales

Michell Gonzales is 21 years old and married to PV2 Gonzales who is 20 years old and serving in Iraq. She is a full time student.

I have a secret that needs to be told. I have a secret that no one knows. After September 11, 2001, I knew that one day we would be at war and that my husband would be sent away. I prepared for this day for months.

In January, there was news of the war in Iraq starting, that soldiers were starting to be deployed. With anticipation and worry of having to say goodbye for the last time, I moved away. The thought of not seeing him again made me sick to my stomach. Moving away and not having to watch him leave, dressed in his desert Battle Dress Uniform, helped me to think that maybe he will return some day. The day he left, I went on with my day as if he just called me with no news. Now I regret that day, I wish I could have been there seeing him off, I wish I could have kissed him once more, to say good bye if he did not return.

These last few months have been hard. At first I didn't think of him much. I didn't watch the news or listen to the radio. After a couple of months, I started having nightmares. In one dream I followed him to a gate, but I couldn't pass the gate because it was blocked with Iraqi soldiers. On the other side of the gate there was fighting, bullets flying through the air and bombs going off. I was being shot at, and I had to get away. But the thing I remember most about that dream was that my husband didn't turn around, he didn't look back, or show me that he was okay. He went on shooting and fighting for his life, and for the lives of his fellow soldiers.

I went on with my life; I went back to school to finish my degree. I thought that getting on with my life was going to take the pain away. Not knowing how or where my husband was, though, it didn't.

I look at people differently today. They go on with their lives like there is nothing going on in the world—that this war is like a leaf that has been blown away. I am alone here. No one knows me; they don't know who I am, and why I am here. They think of me as one of them.

I read once in a poem that another wife had written, "You walk past her on the street, you ring up her groceries at the supermarket, you bank with her. Who is this lady who wears a yellow ribbon on her shirt? She is a mother and a father; she is a gardener and a repairman. She lives her life and doesn't bother anyone, but inside, she is a soldier's wife."

People who do know me don't even think about what I am going through, but, in fact, that is what hurts me the most. People have forgotten what is going on, but not me. I hear the phone ring, and my heart jumps a beat. When the doorbell rings, I wonder who it may be. Sometimes I can hear my husband's voice calling out to me. With hope, I turn and look to see if it may be him, not just a ghost.

Lately, it's gotten harder for me. People close to me have gotten injured or died. My husband wrote in one of his letters that he was depressed and he didn't know how to handle it. This made me angry; angry at the fact that I can't be over there helping him, protecting him. My heart goes out to these men and women, and to my husband. I hurt from the fact that people have forgotten and disregarded the fact that there are still soldiers out there dying. I am broken, broken by the fact that people have to die for our country or get hurt. I am mad that these families have to live every day of their lives without their sons, daughters, husbands, wives, mothers, and fathers. Some nights I don't sleep, some days I don't think. I become invisible to others. I hide my feelings. I am proud of the men and woman who go out and serve to protect all Americans. This is *my* story: I have a secret within me. I am a wife of a soldier who is fighting in Iraq.

"We're just ordinary women with extraordinary experiences.... Me today, perhaps you tomorrow."

Bee Pedersen's son, Kevin, at the homecoming ceremony after a year in Iraq.

"The postal worker looked and smiled at me. 'When will he be back?'"

4th ID soldiers Iraq, 2003

Anxious and Waiting

By Lauren King

Lauren King's National Guard husband was called to active duty January 19, 2003.

When I was growing up, I always wondered what it would be like to know a soldier. I never knew I would be married to one. When I first started dating my husband, he would always go away for a weekend once a month to serve his National Guard duty. He would polish his black boots and make sure he had everything together the night before, so he could just get up and leave.

Before he would leave, he would always make sure to kiss my forehead and tell me that he loved me, and that he would be back on Sunday. I thought that would be all Devin would have to do. I never dreamed of him leaving me behind and going off to war.

When Devin was called up to serve, I just knew it wasn't true, because he only had two days left in the military. I will never forget that night—we both had the night off, and we were playing on the computer and having a great night when his phone rang. It was someone at the armory, but before he even picked it up he said, "Lauren, this is it."

I froze as I watched his facial expressions. I was so scared that I had to walk in the other room and try not to cry. He hung up and made a couple of other phone calls before he got off the phone. We held each other like we never had before. I felt so safe in his arms at that very moment. After September 11, we talked about a possible deployment, but we never thought of Iraq. He was supposed to go guard the border and not leave the country, and I had thought *that* was going to be difficult! I was wrong. I honestly didn't believe that he was really going to Iraq until he started going through his stuff and talking about getting married.

Devin proposed two days before Christmas. I was so excited, but I was a little nervous too, because we had talked about waiting to get married until after he graduated from college. I knew something was up, but he just told me he wanted me to have a ring. Since Devin was called to active duty January 19, 2003, we went ahead and married January 21. We both couldn't believe that we were married because neither of us had been married before. We were both happy, but I knew it meant more serious things, like Devin going to war, and me being here alone with no family. We didn't even get to go on a honeymoon. Devin kept apologizing to me for having to leave. I really hope he knows why he is over there, because there are days when I don't know what the heck we are doing there.

That dreaded morning came to take him to the armory to see him off. It was about 5:45 a.m. I was so tired, and I could tell Devin was, too. I was not ready to say goodbye. I hadn't had enough time with him. I knew this was going to be so hard. I watched as he unpacked his green bag from my car. I was fighting back my tears until he left because I knew he needed me to be strong for him. I tried, but it was hard. I let it all out. I was so terrified: scared for him, for me, and at the thought of not ever seeing him again. I had to reassure myself that Devin is a strong man. I knew he had been to Kuwait, but not to fight a war.

At that moment I felt like I was losing myself. I made myself quit crying. I knew I had to be strong. If Devin was strong, that meant I had to be, too. Before he got out of the car, he said, "Lauren, I love you so much, and please don't forget that." Then he got out of the car and walked away. I will never forget that morning.

Since the deployment, it has been rough. I knew nothing about the military, especially the benefits, and I certainly learned the hard way. I moved into a new apartment while Devin was at Fort Hood, waiting to see if Turkey would let the troops enter there. My mother and brother came to help me move all of our stuff. I thought that Devin wasn't going to be able to see our new apartment until he returned, but they gave the soldiers a chance to return for the weekend to be with their families. I was so excited that we were able to spend the whole weekend together. Even though we just laid around and got the apartment organized, I was so glad we were able to share those special moments together.

Then he left again, and this time, it was really goodbye until he comes home in April 2004. I didn't even get to go to Fort Hood to see him board the airplane. He told me that he might not be able to see me that day, so I didn't go. I really regret that now. He called and told me he loved me and that he would see me soon. Soon was not enough for me; I didn't even want him to leave. He left April 2, 2003. I received a phone call from the airport in Sicily. He sounded so close, as if he were just talking to me from Fort Hood. I wanted to reach out and touch him, but that was not possible. He told me he didn't know when he was going to be able to call again, and I didn't hear his voice again until a couple of months later when I received a message. I had been at work, and he had left a message. It truly made my night. Then the phone calls started coming almost every Sunday or Monday. I tried not to work those days, so that I wouldn't miss his phone calls. When he didn't call, I worried and wondered why—afraid that something had happened.

I have formed some close friendships through all of this. Whenever Tori called to tell me her husband had called and said that they were all okay, I felt so relieved. I knew Devin and his unit were busy, but I just wanted to hear his voice. When he was finally able to call again, it was a late phone call. He made sure I told everyone that he loved them.

August came around, and Devin called to tell me that he'd be coming home around Thanksgiving. I was so excited, but I just couldn't believe it until I saw it. There were so many rumors floating around, and these poor guys believed them. I knew that all they wanted to do was come home. I really got my hopes up, but they deflated when I attended a meeting at the armory and they said it wasn't true. I felt so down and I knew everyone else did, too. I decided I didn't want to live alone anymore. I had no family, and my friends were great—but I couldn't stand to stay around and watch them all go out and party every night. I just wasn't in the mood to do anything while Devin was thousands of miles away. Everyone offered to help me move, but the timing made it difficult for them to come and help, so it was "the crew": my mom, me, and my brother.

I swear we will be "pros" someday. I just wanted to cry every time I thought about Devin not being here on Thanksgiving and Christmas. I would have given anything to have him here with us.

Every day you wake up and look in a newspaper to make sure nothing bad has happened. Or you wait for the doorbell to ring, but you don't want to answer it because they could give you the bad news. It is really a scary feeling. It happened to me once, and I thought I was going to collapse. It was just a salesperson, though.

Much as I want my husband to come home, I am scared to even see Devin. I'm scared of what our reactions are going to be. We will have been apart for a year when he returns. I know people change, and I hope things will still be good between us.

Devin's yearlong deployment has brought me closer to his family, and, it has brought me many close friendships that I will cherish for the rest of my life. God bless America and remember, each and every soldier and their families are all heroes.

"My son James called me; he said he's coming home for a two-week leave. I'm so thrilled but at the same time, I'm so worried. I know that he'll have to go back, and I know that it won't be easy. We all know what will happen if they don't. I've heard that some of them couldn't face going back. For the guys that decide to stay, it will be five years in Leavenworth, I think. This is a very stressful time."

Maj. Gen. Odierno's Veterans' Day Message

From the Ironhorse Desert News, dated November 10, 2003

"As we honor the veterans of past conflicts and the current global war on terrorism, I would like to thank you, the soldiers of Task Force Ironhorse. And as important, I would like to thank your families for the sacrifices and contributions you both have made to this war."

—Courtesy of The Ironhorse Desert News

Daddy's R&R Leave

By Sherri Martin

Sherri Martin's husband, Specialist Alejandro (Alex) Martin, was deployed to Iraq and returned home for R&R. Specialist Martin is with Charlie Company, 124th Signal Battalion, stationed in Balad, Iraq. They live in Ft. Hood, Texas. Sherri is a stay-at-home mom to two children: a two-year old daughter, Julie, and a five-month old son, Josh; born while his daddy was deployed to Iraq.

My **husband is sleeping upstairs with his newborn son** sleeping next to him. Everything is perfect and at peace in our home right now. He came home November 1, 2003, for R&R, and so many amazing things have happened since he's been back. When he came down the stairs at the Austin airport, and I could finally tell our two-year-old daughter to go get her Daddy and I watched her pudgy little legs run up to him with such excitement—that was pure BLISS.

She screamed, "Daddy, Daddy!" and just melted in his arms. Then when I presented his six-week-old son to him, I broke down. I didn't know what to feel. But I suppose it was an eclectic mixture of PRIDE in him for the sacrifices he's made to be over there, LOVE for him because he'd helped make this perfect little life, and COMPLETE JOY because the time had finally come for him to meet his baby boy for the first time. With our daughter in one arm and our son in his other and me happily squished right up with them, we were a family again.

On the ride home, he felt the support of Texas, as people honked at us. I had written on our minivan, "Daddy meets his newborn son today!! Honk if you're happy!" Well, we got honks! Thanks, Texas!

My husband got to get a little taste of my world; more specifically, my nighttime routine. And on that first night home, the kids decided to "tag-team" their cries. Our two-year-old daughter always needed specific blankets and stuffed toys to fall asleep, and would cry if they weren't all present and tucked in, but now she cried hysterically for her daddy as well—she didn't want to let him leave her sight. So Daddy would go into her room and get what she needed, and reassure her that he was going to be there when she woke up the next morning. Finally, she'd settle down. Just as we'd get comfortable in our bed, our little, six-week-old boy would need us. This went on, back and forth, for several hours. My husband asked me, "Do you do this every night, Sherri?"

I looked at him and repeated, "Every night!" He finally understood firsthand why I would be pulling my hair out with tired frustration when he called at night, and why I'd be so completely drained and exhausted when he called in the morning. He has been wonderfully compassionate and understanding from then on. Every night he's happily gotten up with the baby and brought him to me to nurse him or give him a bottle. After a few nights, our daughter stopped crying out for her daddy, and things got easier.

It was funny, but kind of sad, to watch him jump and react to silly things. On his first night here, the tissue box fell off the nightstand, and I swear before it hit the ground, he was ready to defend himself and destroy this enemy! Throughout the night he'd keep waking up to hear the soft ticking and hum of the air conditioner and get very tense, thinking there was an intruder in our home. Despite all my reassurances, he had to investigate the matter and see for himself that all was okay and we were safe. After all, the man of the house was back! The next morning, he opened an unfamiliar door in our new house. It was the closet where I keep the ironing board. He mistook it for a stranger hiding, and drew his arm back to punch the life out of him. I felt so sad that the war, and his time in Iraq, had made him like that, and that soon I'd have to send him away to that place again. The countdown had begun. I knew his time at home would go by so quickly. I already had visions of us saying goodbye at the airport.

Having him here has helped us both in many ways. It's given him a break from the danger and monotony of the day-to-day war in Iraq, as well as a new perspective on raising a two-year-old! It's given me a break from the danger and monotony of really stinky diapers and super-green, super-nasty runny noses. Trying to recover from a C-section while trying to be super mom to the kids has left me feeling like anything but a super mom. My husband's visit has recharged my batteries and given me a chance to get some much-needed rest. It's also let me appreciate how blessed I am that I'll never know firsthand what it is that made him get anxious over a tissue box or punch that ol' ironing board that lurks in our closet....

Curlen Martinson and friend, Iraq, 2003. The Ziggurat (Abraham's House). Built approximately 2400 B.C. Located near Tallil Air Base.

Two soldiers keeping an alert eye on the activities around them

"POW, MIA...who truthfully understands the painful meaning of those abbreviations?"

US Soldiers inside a Chinook.
"My concerns about bills, taxes, and doctor's appointments are so far from this world right now."

Remains likely from '91 uprising

Associated Press, Wednesday, January 7, 2004

A new mass gravesite in Iraq has been discovered recently about 30 miles (48 kilometers) south of Baghdad, U.S. officials said Wednesday.

About 800 victims from the Shiite Muslims' 1991 failed uprising against Saddam are believed to be buried at the southern Iraq site. Without the support of coalition forces that had driven Saddam out of Kuwait in the Persian Gulf War, the uprising was crushed and thousands killed.

U.S. officials said they have identified about 670 mass gravesites across the country.

Happy Holidays????

By Margaret Conrad Hodges

Born and raised in Cornwall NY, Margaret Hodges went into the Air Force when she was 17, met and married her husband, Rob in 1984, near the end of her 4-year enlistment as he was finishing technical school. As an Explosive Ordnance Disposal technician, he deploys often. They are stationed at Aviano Air Base, Italy, but previously were at Shaw AFB, South Carolina, where her husband was involved in the preparation for the war in Iraq. He deployed to Qatar in November and has teams in Iraq, Afghanistan, and places she says she can't pronounce. She is a secretary at Aviano. Their son, Anthony, turns 18 in March and graduates in June!

During the hustle and bustle of the season, let's not forget that there are people who will not have family or loved ones around during the holidays. While you celebrate Hanukah, Kwanza, or Christmas—or even if you are not celebrating, but just enjoying winter—there are people who are living in tents, sleeping on the ground, taking fire from people we're supposedly there to help, and surrounded by death and disease. And there are more people who are left behind to worry and wait.

This is not new. There is always a mission, whether military or humanitarian, that takes our families away from safety and away from home during this time of year. Remember them while you're impatiently stuck in traffic. Remember them when you're standing in extra-long lines behind carts loaded down with gifts and goodies. Remember them when you've had too much dinner or too much dessert and can't get comfortable in front of your television. Remember them when you just can't seem to find the right dress or the right tie for yet another holiday gathering.

At such times, remember the ones who are loaded down with their weapons, flak vests, and helmets. Remember the ones who have to stand in long lines to take a shower—something they cherish, as they don't always get to take one every day. Remember the ones who stand in long lines to get indistinguishable food just to nourish them and carry them through another day, if they get hot food at all. Remember the ones who may or may not get a card or letter with holiday greetings or news from home, because they are always on the move to defend someone whose rights and lives are in danger. And remember the families and loved ones, parents, spouses, and children they left behind.

Remember the young wife who is expecting a child, who hasn't heard from her husband in weeks and isn't even sure where he is. Remember the mother of the young soldier as she lies awake at night praying and hoping for her son's or daughter's safe return. Remember the children of the soldiers, sailors, and airmen—they aren't sure why their parent is gone to such a scary far-away place, but they know they have one less bedtime hug, or one less hand to hold, or perhaps one less parent. Remember the communities that are without a piece of their heart and soul because some of their citizens are serving the best nation in the world and helping nations less fortunate than ours to realize freedom and happiness. Please remember, and silently wish them well.

We are stationed at Aviano Air Base Italy—the same base from which, just last March, over 10,000 Army troops were airlifted to the desert. We tried very hard to show them the respect and hospitality they deserved. Apparently we did a fair job of it, as they have not yet stopped talking about their stay here. My husband is working in Qatar and Iraq, and hopefully, he and his team will all return to Italy safely and the rest of our troops will return home safely, too!

As the wife of a 20-year Air Force explosive ordnance disposal technician serving in the desert this holiday season, and mother of a 17-year-old son who intends to serve his country, I don't let a moment go by without wishing our troops a safe return home. I served in the Air Force during the Cold War, as it was called, but that was considered a time of peace. This is not our first holiday apart, nor will it be our last.

I just think it's about time the rest of the world realized that the sacrifices our troops make to defend their freedoms and the freedoms of others, and the sacrifices their families make as well, are worth each person taking just a moment in their busy lives to wish them well and a safe return home.

"Jeff finally made it home!!! I thought that this morning would never occur. I had tried to imagine what it would feel like, but it was more overwhelming that I ever would have thought. I cried and cried, I just couldn't stop. He looks so grown up, and yet he's only 19. For the first time in eight months I'll be able to relax and sleep."

Bradley Fighting Vehicle in front of Saddam Hussein's birthday palace, Tikrit, Iraq. Hundreds of US soldiers stayed here and slept side by side during Operation Iraqi Freedom.

Soldiers

Angela C. Rooney

Heather J. Williams

Karah McNeill

Digna Maria Vargas-Yarbrough and family

Curlen M. Martinson

Pamela A. Morris

Pearletta Beth Ullrich

Soldiers

Wolfowitz Salutes Women's 'Spectacular Display of Military Professionalism'

By Gerry J. Gilmore, American Forces Press Service

WASHINGTON, May 9, 2003—Today's military women are dedicated professionals who play key roles across America's armed services, U.S. Deputy Defense Secretary Paul D. Wolfowitz told members of DoD's military women's advisory group.

America's military women, have provided important contributions—often while in harm's way—in support of recent military operations, Wolfowitz today told members of the Defense Advisory Committee on Women in the Services.

—Courtesy American Forces Press Service

My Words

By Angela C. Rooney

Staff Sergeant Angela C. Rooney, U.S. Air Force, was deployed to Kuwait right before Operation Iraqi Freedom started. Angela Rooney grew up in Cedar Falls, Iowa. She entered the U.S. Air Force in 1997, and works in the supply career field. She is married to Phillip, who is also a staff sergeant serving in the Air Force. They are expecting their first baby in April 2004.

March 2003

Tonight I sleep in my uniform. I'm dirty from a day of building tents with the sand blowing in every direction. A film of sand constantly covers me. If sand were good for the skin, I would be in facial heaven. But they say wearing our uniforms will give us more protection if we're attacked by chemicals. So we all go to bed wearing some form of the uniform. It isn't that uncomfortable, and I feel a lot safer. With my gas mask next to my bed and my chemical warfare suit open and ready to go, I feel that much closer to safety, and that much farther from reality.

The war is going to start any night now. I can hear helicopters and aircraft overhead. I see dark figures running through the night. They tell us there isn't shelter for us to take if we start getting hit by Saddam's regime, so we're to stay in our tents if SCUDs begin to fly. STAY IN OUR TENTS??? And this wind-beaten piece of canvas is supposed to save us? I think not.

So, all the girls in my tent, all ten of us, have come up with a plan. (I suspect all the tents have a plan in case things start to hit the fan.) One of the girls living in my tent has the keys to a CONEX box right outside our tent door, so we plan to take cover in it. We all have light sticks because the camp is dark at night, and we'll need light when trying to hurry to the CONEX. But we are never hit with SCUDs. We are so fortunate; Kuwait was hit several times.

We huddle around the lone TV to watch the news during the day. We can't call home and can't write letters, so we are forced to just pray and hope our families are doing okay. It must be hard on them not to know how we are and not to be able to talk to us. We are at a classified location in the middle of a war and have no outside communication. It isn't the easiest thing I have ever had to achieve.

Days turn to weeks and weeks turn to months. Most days are the same. The nights are short, and the days are long—filled with erecting tent city and keeping this place running. We eat MREs (meals, ready to eat) for all three meals a day and haven't seen a flush toilet in months. Forget dreaming about shopping malls and fancy restaurants. All I want is a fork to eat with and a mattress to sleep on.

The nationals let us borrow their shower room, but that consists of a cold drizzle of contaminated water. The nationals wash their feet in the sinks so those are definitely off limits to us, or at least, we made them off limits. The nationals don't want girls using their shower room, so we must take combat showers in order for us all to get through in the time limit they gave us. Not that we want to hang out in the filth and grime of their facilities anyway.

They are trying to improve the morale here at the camp, so we are doing something besides eating, working, and sleeping. Somehow a film projector was acquired from one of the cargo planes (nobody ever knows what will come in on the cargo planes—it's like Christmas every time one lands). So they started projecting movies onto the side of a semi truck and we sit outside and watch movies at night when the work is done for the day. It's a definite plus, since this is the only thing we have to do here. We are often so tired, though, that not having any entertainment is fine with all of us. We appreciate the effort, though.

The friends we make here are ones to last a lifetime. Friends are your backbone when you think you can't stand it any longer. They know your ins and outs, and accept you for what you are. We are all in the same situation here, and we all help each other out. We have wonderful times just chit-chatting about life back home with our families and friends. All of us were sent here not knowing anyone, but have gained a new family from the life experiences and challenges that arise.

Through 150 days together, at the various locations that we deployed to, the friends I worked with and the friends I lived with are who I thank for keeping me going. This was the toughest challenge I have ever had to endure, and I survived it because of them. They will be in my heart forever.

First Sergeant Heather Williams and Iraqi workers, Baghdad.
"This was my first assignment as a Group First Sergeant."

"I can't believe it, James just got the results. He got the Baghdad boil/leishmaniasis. He got it from these bastard sand flies out there. I did send him the flea collars, but as you remember, we were told they were harmful for people."

From College to Combat

By Karah McNeill

Twenty-two-year-old Karah McNeil, Airman First Class, U.S. Air Force, spent three months in Kuwait; the base that was the closest installation to Iraq at that time. Karah McNeil is currently stationed at Ellsworth Air Force Base, South Dakota, where she edits the base newspaper.

Here I was, gigantic leg and all. My left leg looked more like a student's art project than a leg. My knee was twice its usual size, and every hour a nurse would come and draw a line around the infection with a ballpoint pen. This enabled the doctors to map the progression of my mystery infection. At 22, I'd never imagined that I'd be in a temporary hospital in the middle of the desert. I can't recall ever smelling worse than I did that week. I had spent three days in my chemical protection gear because I wasn't able to put it on and get to a shelter in time to avoid a possible biological attack. But I guess I'm getting ahead of myself....

To understand my view of the war on Iraq, you must first take a peak into my past. I didn't come from a military family, nor did I ever have a strong military influence in my life. I did, however, come from a very strong and patriotic family. But when it came to thinking about my future, serving my country never came to mind. I never doubted that I could "hack it" out there with the boys, but I had no desire to work on jets or sleep in the sand.

I attended a private university and was a double major in mass media and communications. I wanted to be involved in media or public relations, although I wasn't too sure how. I was also being pursued by a sorority, and was on the verge of pledging. In order to afford my expensive tuition as a full-time student and my active social life, I worked two jobs. I was just your typical college girl.

On September 11, 2001, I woke up like I did every day and went to the optometry office where I'd worked for the past year. As the day progressed, I caught little tidbits of what was happening.

It wasn't until that evening that I was able to sit and take in the entire horrifying scene. I cried and I instantly knew I'd have to get involved somehow. In the following weeks I decided that my contribution would be to serve my country. I entered Air Force basic training in February of 2002 at the age of 21.

After receiving my training in public affairs, I knew that I had done the right thing. I was a military journalist, still doing what I had set out to do in college but doing my part for freedom as well.

When I arrived at my first assignment, before I even set my things down, I was informed that I would be going to Southwest Asia. I was excited and nervous at the same time. Most people aren't shipped out so soon after arriving, but because I was going to assist by escorting foreign workers onto the air base, the normal guidelines were waived.

On December 21, 2002, I found myself on a plane flying over the Atlantic Ocean en route to Kuwait. The base where I'd spend the next three months was the closest installation to Iraq at the time.

I felt like I'd been dropped in a foreign country without a map or translator. Because I had never been around military people, I didn't know the lingo or how things were supposed to be done. Granted, I had been taught everything I needed to know in basic training, but I hadn't really had any time to practice safety precautions. And in my frightened state, I couldn't recall any of it.

I must not have been alone, because we had routine drills to make sure that if the need arose we could perform the necessary safety measures and walk away unharmed.

It took me about a month to get accustomed to the way things work on a base at the front line. Before I knew it, though, I was briefing my squadron on the decontamination process. I felt confident in my ability to protect myself and those around me while still performing my necessary, everyday tasks.

As an escort, I met people from a dozen different countries. Some had come to Kuwait because their country was very poor and they couldn't provide for their families any other way. I also met quite a few members from allied nations. The experiences shared during these conversations were phenomenal. If I'd ever doubted my decision, the stories I heard were enough to shake some sense into me.

The week before the war kicked off, I became sick. I mysteriously developed an infection in my left knee and was hospitalized. They couldn't subdue the infection, so I had to be constantly hooked to an IV.

One day, without notice, the alarms began to sound. All of a sudden, a loudspeaker instructed everyone to run to a bunker or hardened shelter immediately. I could barely wobble to the restroom, let alone run. I was horrified. My IV was hastily removed, and I was being ushered out of the hospital before I knew what was happening. Two Army guys with similar debilitating leg wounds hobbled with me to a shelter. I spent the next hour in chemical protection gear and gas mask.

During many of the exercises when I sat in a bunker sweating in my gas mask, I wondered how I'd react if it were ever a real situation. Many people experience anxiety attacks or claustrophobia in gas masks. The first time was more surprising than scary, so I didn't really get around to freaking out. Ten minutes after we'd been released from the shelter, we were told to run again. It was then that I understood there weren't going to be any more exercises. Everyone jumped into wartime mode and the games were over.

Despite this mystery disease and the alarms, I was more worried about my family than I was about myself. I knew that my mother was glued to the television watching round-the-clock news coverage of the inevitable war. I knew that she didn't want to be there watching, but it was like a scab—she couldn't help picking at it.

During the first two days of the war the alarms became routine. About every three hours, the two Army guys and I found ourselves helping each other out the hospital door to the shelter. These were the most surreal moments of my life. I thought I'd be panicking in the face of real danger, but instead, we played games of "Simon Says" and sang childhood songs to keep our minds off the loud noise outside.

As a member of the Air Force, I was definitely among the privileged. I wasn't on the front lines like my Army and Marine brothers and sisters. I was sitting in a shelter on a heavily guarded base, miles away from any gunfights. As the week wore on, the alarms became fewer and fewer, and I was finally able to take that much-needed shower.

Sunday, March 23, 2003, was my dad's birthday, and it was also the day I was told I was going home. Service members from the front line needed to be shipped to the closest hospital, and I was taking up a much-needed bed. I've never felt so thrilled, sad, and guilty all at once.

After three months in the desert, I was happy because my mother would stop growing gray hairs, and I'd see my loving boyfriend and family again. But I also felt incredibly guilty because some of my comrades on the front lines would spend many more months in the extreme weather. And of those who'd later return, some wouldn't come back alive.

Some of my Marine and Army friends are now facing the enemy, and I find myself feeling a bit left out. I definitely had a sheltered view of the war, but this experience opened my eyes. I grew up and saw more in those three months than I had in my entire life.

"Every now and then, though, it hits me. This is war. He can die. I say those words again. He can die. It's a fact I only seem to realize when I'm alone, finishing up some work for the next day. It comes out of nowhere, really. I just roll over on my bed and start sobbing."

U.S. Forces detain 400 Iraqis in a Large-Scale Roundup

By David Rohde, with Michael Gordon

The New York Times, June 11, 2003, Thuluiya, Iraq—American forces completed their largest combat operation in Iraq since the fall of Baghdad today, with more than 3,000 soldiers backed by fighter jets, armored vehicles and patrol boats surrounding a 30-square mile peninsula north of Baghdad that is said to harbor gunmen attacking American soldiers.

All of This Packed into 20 Years

By Digna Maria Vargas-Yarbrough

Specialist Digna Maria Vargas-Yarbrough has been in the military for two years. She is attached to the 4th Infantry Division as a Russian linguist. She has been married for one year to a soldier in the 3rd Infantry Division, who also has been deployed to Iraq.

Digna Maria's parents, Nancy and Carlos, live in Florida. Her father is in the Air Force Reserve and served five months in Iraq. Her brother, Carlos, plans on attending the Air Force Academy. Brother-in-law Joe served seven months in Iraq with the 3rd Infantry Division. Digna Maria's mother works for the Civilian Personnel Office at Pensacola Air Force Base.

1420 Hours, 01 DEC 2003

Hello, my familia,

I'm writing this letter for a few reasons: (a) to let you know that our new location has no Internet or phones (b) to tell you that we made it safely to our new locale, and (c) that I'm doing well. Hopefully, I'll be able to get to a phone/computer soon and then you'll know all of this before this letter gets to you. In the event that you get this letter first, just know that I'm *really* sorry that I can't make contact, and that I'm perfectly fine.

So, how are things with you guys? Work and school going well? Are there any new developments that I should know about? What kinda tree did y'all put up/are you going to put up? Depending on when you get this is what'll determine whether it's actually up (16 Dec).

Before I forget, can you send legal-sized envelopes and a bag of gummy bears? A pound or two, and some peanut M&Ms would be cool. I have an extravagant request; if the PX/BX sells Godiva chocolate, can you please send the chocolate raspberry truffle? It's dark chocolate with raspberry filling. I promise I'll pay you back. If you could send some of those, mmm, they're so tasty! If you don't find them there, it's no big deal, but thanks a bunch for trying. Oh, and one more thing: a #2 from McDonald's, super-sized w/Sprite! j/k!

Hey, guess what?! A surprise promotion interrupted my letter writing. Guess whose it was…5…4…3…2…1… a girl named DIGNA! Yes, folks, I am a SPECIALIST now. E-4, baby. And, two months before the 24-month mark, which means my Sergeant First Class put in a waiver, which means he thinks I'm an okay soldier. So now, everyone on my team is an E-4 and above, which is pretty cool.

So here's my new endeavour/endeavor (spelling?) adventure/ thing I wanna do. I was thinking of buying a camcorder, but I'm not sure yet. I thought it'd be cool to send you tapes of me and the country and my team and stuff. It's really only a thought, but let me know what you think. I've got two full cameras now, so I'm really gonna try to send photos this week. I can't promise good quality on all of them cause one camera didn't have a built-in flash, and I know that I took pictures in not-so-well-lit places.

So do you think you could send a *huge* box, so that I can send myself home? That'd be swell. We should be outta here soon. Ironically, I can't wait to get home so that I can just sit and watch the grass grow. That would actually be something that I haven't seen in a while. Mostly cause there's no grass here … just sand and weeds. Yeah, so I'd like to SAWTGG (sit and watch the grass grow), swim, SAWTGG, eat, SAWTGG, and have Tito drive me around; I don't care where. All I know is that he's driving!

In the "hopefully-not" event that I can't call soon, mama, I hope you have a wonderfully splendid birthday. There are a bazillion good days in a life, and I hope that this one is extra special. I pray for you all daily and love you all very, very much. You're a *big* chunk of me and the most special people that I know. I'm anxious to get back home to put the "chunks" together again. Please take care of yourselves and know that I love you all very much. I'm sending a humongous hug with this letter, so please share it (the hug), with all of my other "chunks."

Xoxoxoxoxox…love, your daughter and sister,

Digna Maria Vargas-Yarbrough

A time to grieve: Family, friends mourn Hood soldier killed in Iraq

By Juan A. Lozano

The Associated Press, Houston—At the end of her daughter's funeral, Armandina Gutierrez de Esparza clutched a white dove, then gently let it fly away. Twenty other doves then were released from a cage Wednesday in tribute to Pfc. Analaura Esparza Gutierrez, who last week became the second female combat fatality among four U.S. women soldiers killed in Iraq.

Weekend Warrior

By Melissa Lyn Neely

Melissa Lyn Neely is a Staff Sergeant in the Air Force Reserve. On February 15, 2003, her unit started to out-process to go to Qatar. She was born and raised in Pennellville, New York. Her parents are Ronald and Patricia Stiles. She currently resides in Newport News, Virginia with her husband, Sheldon. She has a BA in Public Justice with a minor in Forensics.

Many people make fun of the Guard and Reserve. They say that all of them are weekend warriors, which is far from the truth. My name is Melissa Lyn Neely, and I am far more than a weekend warrior. I am a Staff Sergeant in the Air Force Reserve, a wife, a daughter, a sister, an aunt, a godmother, a goddaughter, a friend, and a co-worker—and this is a short account of my experience over the past year.

I was married in May 2002, and shortly thereafter, activated to go and support homeland defense in Florida. This wasn't bad, due to the fact I was still able to see my husband occasionally during those months. I returned to my home in Virginia at the end of October, just in time for Halloween. I went to my part-time job at the mall, and after the holidays I started to interview for a full-time position with the Hampton Police Department. That was put on hold when the call came from my unit in New York stating I had 72 hours to report. I was deploying overseas. This happened on February 12, 2003.

On February 15, my unit started to out-process to go to Qatar. Our orders were cut for a year. My family, who live in New York, came to see me off: my parents, my grandparents, my aunt and uncle, my sister and her two girls, and my cousins, and their daughter and son, who is also my godson. I had the biggest send-off of my entire unit. My father, a master sergeant in the Air Force, asked all of my fellow guardsmen, who have known him for years, to look out for me while we are over there. And they all did.

After too many hours of traveling, we arrived at our destination.

In Doha International Airport, we all grabbed the sea of green bags. We proceeded through customs and rode a bus to Al Udeid. In the early morning, we settled into our tents. Day in and day out we had the same routine: wake up, eat, go to work for 12-16 hours a day, go to the gym, go to bed, and do it all over again.

I was very lucky when I was over there. Almost every day I received something from home, whether it was a letter or a package full of goodies to share. When you are in strange surroundings, it is great to get a little piece of home. The first letter I received was from my seven-year-old niece wishing that I would be home in time for my first anniversary. I wished the same thing. I had all of my letters displayed on a wall by my computer. Even though I worked nights, they brightened my day every time I looked at them.

We were not allowed to call home while the campaign was going on, and e-mail was our only link to our families. Thank God for technology. Around the beginning of April, we were allowed one call per week to our family. I was so happy to hear my husband's voice, and he mine. My parents felt relieved as well.

At the end of April, we got the word we were going home. I couldn't believe it. First the possibility of having to stay for a year, and now all of a sudden we were going home. I thought it was too good to be true, but lo and behold, in the beginning of May, I arrived back in New York. My husband would not be able to take leave until May 17, so I would have to wait patiently. The most extraordinary thing about the day I came back was the fact that I came home on my niece's christening. She had prayed every night that I would be able to come back before my first anniversary, and her prayer came true.

The look of surprise and sheer happiness on my niece's face was priceless. It was enough to make everything I'd done worthwhile. She was so happy, and she couldn't believe that I was standing in her living room. She gave me the biggest hug ever. We had cake and a small get-together with my family that night. I was home!

After all of the dinners and get-togethers, visits to some local schools, and in-processing at the base, my husband was able to get leave and come see me. And he had a huge surprise—he bought me a brand-new 2003 Grand Prix! I was speechless. And to top it off, we had our anniversary dinner at the same place where we had our wedding reception only a year earlier. It was a night to remember.

I was still not used to being back in the States. It felt strange to see grass and trees and water everywhere. I didn't have to brush my teeth with bottled water or walk a couple of blocks to use the rest room. Even today there are a few things that I am not used to. I am still trying to settle in. I still even have a bag or two to unpack.

I am back in Virginia now, working full-time as an IMA at Langley Air Force Base. I still remember my time in the desert, and I think of it fondly—it was a priceless experience with top-notch people. We all came together for our country in a time of war. I worked with the Air Force, Army, and Navy, including active duty, Guard, and Reserve. Some people had been retired for a year and called back to duty. Some were police officers, lawyers, students—you name it.

Obviously, the Guard and Reserve are not just weekend warriors— far from it. The schedule of one weekend a month and two weeks a year doesn't exist anymore. I can only hope that when you think of all the men and women that are still over there, you pray for their safe and speedy return. Just imagine that for every solider on duty there is a parent, a spouse, or a child hoping and praying to see their loved one standing in their living room, longing for that awaited hug.

"Dearest sister, we miss you so much and pray that you'll be home very soon. We are planning the wedding and hope you can make it back by then. Love you so much."

Camp PA 101 Airborne, Iraq.
A soldier is getting his head shaved.

101 Airborne, Mosul, Iraq, 2003.
"Several times for the last few months, we have been called out only for painful false alarms. This time it's for real... my son is going to war."

A Desert Nurse

By Tammy Dunham

Tammy Dunham is from Jamestown, Ohio. Tammy was deployed to Saudi Arabia, February-May 2003, and Iraq, May-July 2003, for Operations Southern Watch, Enduring Freedom, Iraqi Freedom, and Desert Scorpion. Her family includes husband, Jon, and daughter, Courtney.

"Lieutenant Dunham, you need to pack your bags and be ready to leave by this afternoon. You are being sent to Iraq."

I had been at a base in Saudi Arabia since February, alternating my work time between a ward and a clinic. Now it was May—after the President declared major fighting over—and I was going to Iraq. These words changed my whole deployment. In the space of one phone call, I went from being at a supporting base to joining one on the front. So I packed my bags and readied myself to go to this new place, both scared and excited about what lay ahead.

We arrived at our destination two days later, close to midnight. It was dark, hot, and dusty. We were scared and didn't know what to expect. As we rode in the bus to our camp we could see lights from various tent encampments. We met the Commander at the medical tents, where he talked to us. He told us we were now a part of the first expeditionary medical group in Iraq, the most forward deployed of any combat medical group in the history of the Air Force. He said we would be working hard, but he would not keep us a day more then we needed to be there. He gave us the day off to settle into our tents.

I was assigned to work the ward. I was promoted to the rank of captain my first day of work, one of a select group of people promoted in the country during a time of conflict. I just wanted to work, but the Commander wanted a little ceremony. It will always be a memorable day.

Being in Iraq in July is not something that is easily replicated in the United States. The only place with comparable heat and dust conditions is Death Valley, California. The average daily temperature was 125 degrees Fahrenheit. The Schmal winds occurred daily—30-50 knot winds that would just blow dust everywhere, including into every little pore of your skin. The wind also made the tents flap like they were going to blow away. The second day there we did get a sprinkle of rain, which dried as soon as it hit the ground. We did not receive any direct enemy fire that we were aware of. We had excellent security, and our camp was considered safe and secure for the area. Our water was non-potable, meaning you could use it to wash your clothes and self, but not brush your teeth, drink, or use it to cook. Our camp had wild, rabid dogs that ran through it, bats around the lights at night, and a plethora of insect life. I don't recall one shower that I did not share with a cricket. Of concern to public health were the mosquitoes and sand flies that carry malaria and leishmaniasis, respectively. This required some self-education so that I could watch for signs and symptoms of these diseases in my patients.

These were the conditions under which we received our patients. To offer effective treatment, we had to be quite ingenious at times. Our patients usually arrived dirty, along with being sick or hurt. We all pooled our care packages to make sure these soldiers could have toothbrushes, toothpaste, combs, feminine products, soap, and deodorant during their stay with us. One patient told me that this was the first bath with water he'd had in three weeks. Privacy in the open ward became an issue of sorts with female patients when the doctors needed to do exams. We put up curtains in one area for privacy.

Infection control is an interesting concept in these conditions, requiring a lot of creativity. We had a total of three wards: two medical/surgical and one ICU. The toilet facilities consisted of two port-a-johns, one female and one male. At one point, we had one ward dedicated as an acute gastroenteritis ward. To help avoid spreading disease to others, we curtained off an area of this tent and put a bedside commode in it for these patients to use. We kept our active tuberculosis case in an isoshelter, doors open, with an attendant sitting outside. When we provided direct patient care, we put on the appropriate personal protective gear.

While our tents had environmental control units, the hotter it got during the day, the warmer the tents became, in spite of these wonderful units. Patients with high temperatures or heat-related injuries definitely tested the resourcefulness of the staff. Patients often arrived at the emergency room with core body temperatures of 104 degrees Fahrenheit and greater. They would be stripped of their clothing, sprayed with water, fanned, covered with wet towels, packed with ice, and treated symptomatically. Also, patients were given acetaminophen. Some had such high core temperatures and low Glasgow scales, which determines neurological function, that they were incubated. Stable patients were moved to the ward. The incubated and more unstable patients, such as those with potassium imbalances, were moved to the ICU. Since the majority of these patients arrived in the afternoon, I arranged my schedule to have all nursing and extra duties done by lunch, if possible, to prepare for the large influx of patients in the afternoon.

The medical group I worked with did not provide care for refugees or nationals, but we did care for government-contracted people who were from the region. Speaking through a translator, most expressed appreciation for their care. I always asked specifically if they had a problem with female nurses. All I asked said, "no." Another major concern was making sure that all visitors and patients stepping into our facility were not carrying or wearing loaded weapons. This issue affected our position in the war, because the Geneva Convention specifies that medical facilities cannot have loaded weapons inside.

Medical supplies seemed to be either over-or under-stocked. At one time, we had boxes of thermometer probes for the thermometers we did not have, but no probes for the thermometers we had. Eventually, we acquired the needed supplies. We used boxes covered with blankets for elevating extremities, and also for elevating the head of the cots that were broken. We received supplies from bases that were closing in the region, which meant we did surprisingly well on supplies. Unfortunately, we had more boxes than staff to unpack and stock, and no room for stocking items, so if you wanted something specific that was not used every day and unpacked, you had to go look through the boxes. For a dressing change that needed 3-inch kerlix, I took 6-inch and cut it. We had boxes and boxes of 6-inch kerlix, and we didn't find the 3-inch until the next day. The other unfortunate thing about leaving lots of supplies sitting in boxes was the heat. The temperatures were so hot they ruined many of the supplies, especially the temperature-sensitive drugs. As time went on, we did receive a couple of refrigerators with freezers. We put drinking water and IV fluid bags in these for the patients. We used the frozen IV bags for ice packs, but did not reuse those for actual IVs.

Nutritional medicine proved to be a challenge, since specialized diets were limited. The easiest specialized diet was clear liquid. Again, we pooled our care packages and brought in tea bags, soup, and whatever we could find that would be appropriate for the patients. The hardest diet was a 2200-calorie diabetic diet for a newly diagnosed diabetic. We had what is called unit-grade rations—basically, the military prepackaged meals put in larger containers so they could be fixed for a group instead of an individual. To the best of their ability, the patients ate these meals with us. The ambulatory patients who didn't have IV fluids running were given a meal pass to eat at the dining tent. Through Dining Services, the nursing assistants arranged take-out meals for the non-ambulatory patients.

Returning patients to their units upon discharge was like treasure hunting at times. Not all units had phones. Some units were in convoys. Some units were days away. Patients would sometimes get rides from visitors going their way; others waited overnight for transport. Those with units close by sometimes had to walk to return to their units. Sometimes we had phone numbers for them, and could arrange transportation back to their units. These were the things that my group and I dealt with daily.

Our commander told us, at one of our weekly meetings, that we did things on a daily basis that most military hospitals may only manage once a year. I just focused on taking care of these patients the best I could with what I was given, without thinking of how I felt. I tried to stay positive and not dwell on what the conditions were like, especially since many had it much worse than we did.

When it came time to leave, I knew that others were coming to take my place and the work would be continued. New eyes also might see where more improvements can be made, so things will keep getting better as replacement cycles arrive. Now that I am home, any news about my former region and the patients I cared catches my attention. I am also working through my feelings now about what I saw, and how the others and I lived and worked. I am glad for the opportunity to serve my country with my service to these soldiers. I gave some, but others gave all so we can enjoy our lives today with the freedoms we embrace.

"Yes, it is true that war brings poverty, death, and desolation, but we both believe that—apart from politics and media—some conceptual and life changes will come out of all this devastation and destruction."

A Weekend in Baghdad

By Pfc. L.A. Salinas, I MEFCE

CENTCOM NEWS STORY, April 28, 2003
CIVIL MILITARY OPERATIONS CENTER, BAGHDAD—
As the Iraqi regime continues to crumble, citizens around the country are showering American forces with praises and some protest.

Along with the smiling faces welcoming American military forces there are also hostile activities going on throughout the city. Looting is still present in certain areas. Demonstrations and small arms firing are still going on daily.

The Marines from 3rd Civil Affairs Group make up the Civilian Military Operation Center based out of the Palestine Hotel located in the capital city. They have the mission of helping the people of Iraq take control of Baghdad after the fall of the previous regime.

—Courtesy of CENTCOM NEWS

Live from Baghdad International Airport, Iraq

By Heather J. Williams

First Sergeant Heather J. Williams, 447th Air Expeditionary Group, is deployed to Iraq waiting to get back home. Heather was born in Trinidad, West Indies, and came to U.S. when she was 12 years old. She has been in the Air Force for 23 years and is currently stationed at Luke Air Force Base, Arizona. She has a 18-year-old daughter.

Anticipation

My anticipation came from a series of firsts. This was my first deployment, although I had been on two remote assignments. Of course, this would be different because it was a combat zone, and I would experience actual hostile fire instead of participation in exercises. This was my first time in the Middle East, and, as with any new environment, you have to acclimate. This was my first assignment as a Group First Sergeant, with more than two junior First Sergeants to mentor (I had a total of eight). I also encountered my first tent city living, working, and dining arrangement, my first helicopter and C130 rides, my first full mobility gear for the majority of my day and night, and my first bombs up—close and personal—with many more firsts to follow.

A week before I left, my commander and his wife were gracious enough to have a small dinner party for me, and invited the two junior first sergeants and their families. It seemed strange that they all offered input from their experiences, and it all seemed very negative. I took into account that they were trying to prepare me for the worst, which was good; however, I did not allow their experiences to deter my positive outlook on my upcoming adventures in Baghdad.

I can recall the day I left my home station: Luke Air Force Base, Arizona. It was in the afternoon on Halloween. I was leaving behind my daughter, who had just started her freshman year at Arizona State University. I would be gone for 120 days. To this day, my daughter does not know my exact location because I want her to focus on school instead of the news in Iraq. The conversations with my mom and sisters resulted in expressions of great concern, and one sister cried uncontrollably. I reassured her of my safety, and it seemed to work. My dad, on the other hand, could not be soothed, so his promise to me was to avoid the news from the Middle East until I returned.

The flight to Baltimore Washington International was uneventful, for the most part. It felt weird to realize that I could get through security with a weapon. People were very conscious of this fact; this was apparent from their quizzical looks.

Nothing appeared out of the ordinary until I arrived in Al Udeid. I remember feeling frightened because everything that I knew to be familiar was out of focus. Now I would have to rely on the old adage, "Fake it till you make it." I am a First Sergeant (protector of the troops), and needed to appear confident for the young troops who were about to embark on this new adventure with me. Most of their eyes reminded me of deer in the headlights, and though my faith was working overtime, I am certain that I appeared that way to them as well.

There is a commercial that has a little jingle with a lady singing a chorus of "An-ti-ci-pa-tion is making me wait" and that is exactly what we did: wait, and anticipate. It was dark outside, and the activity around me was loud and jarring. Wisdom, however, has taught me that the unknown is always frightening. After what seemed like forever, I retrieved my eight large bags and boarded a C130 to Baghdad International Airport. The flight was rough, noisy, and long. It may have been a 10-minute flight, but because of all the activity in the sky, I was reminded of the Fourth of July on a really old and rocky roller coaster.

The last part of my anxiety was, of course, my living arrangements. I had been informed that I would be rooming with several officers. Never having lived in a tent before, I did not, and could not, imagine what it would be like. The tent was actually a good size, and each of us had our own space. We were much better off than those in most of the other tents, which housed eight to ten occupants.

Experience of a Lifetime

During my first few days, it was difficult adjusting to sleeping with an air conditioner noise ten times louder than my unit at home. And when I thought that it could not get any worse, the helicopters joined in with night missions. My tent mates, who had endured the noise for almost 120 days and were preparing to rotate, told me that I would adjust. At the time, I thought that no way would I ever be able to adjust to all of these loud, unfamiliar sounds that initially prevented me from sleeping. However, by the fourth day of working 14-16 hours per day I cherished my tent and my twin-size bed, and I became totally oblivious of the noise for four to six hours of sleep.

Another more serious adjustment was getting up in the morning with a full bladder and having to walk a quarter of a mile to the toilet tent. This was the longest quarter of a mile I had ever experienced. I know this was not good for my bladder, and I will probably have to wear Depends a few years sooner than expected!

After being a First Sergeant for over six years, I have encountered a myriad of personnel issues. However, nothing prepared me for the hardships many of the troops dealt with on deployments. Leaving behind family and friends is difficult, and even more so during all the major holidays. The most dreaded part of my day was answering the calls from the Red Cross, because they inevitably led to sadness and disappointment. I frequently became the bearer of bad news because a grandparent passed away or a wife miscarried. But due to circumstances, in most instances, emergency leave was not an option.

Though we had an obvious enemy, the squadron First Sergeants and I practiced conflict resolution on a daily basis due to close quarters, inconsistent work schedules, and sanitation problems. Fear was responsible for the majority of the behavior problems we encountered, yet I had to instill a "mission first" attitude and keep a watchful eye to help the troops through the process. After a rocket hit the campsite, I took charge and directed hundreds of troops to a safe zone. I was scared out of my wits, yet I also felt a sense of strength and purpose that controlled my instincts and reactions.

My time in Iraq was not all doom and gloom; there were many positive experiences as well. For instance, I had the distinct pleasure of rubbing elbows with more celebrities in four months than I have in my entire 42 years of living. Enjoying all the special treats and mail from schools, churches, squadrons, and other organizations was encouraging and welcome too. I am grateful for all the hot meals, exercise machines, supplies, and equipment that we had—I can only imagine what it must have been like to go to a bare base. There is much to be thankful for. I was a daily eyewitness of "the rocket's red glare, the bombs bursting in air" that gave me proof each night that our flag was still there.

In addition to my normal First Sergeant responsibilities, I routinely worked with different committees in the camp, creating events and activities for the younger troops. Bingo seemed to be the most popular social event. Every Sunday at 1800, large groups of camp residents sat with their two bingo cards waiting to be the next big winner of a DVD or portable CD player, and how about that grand prize of the ever-popular X-BOX? Each week the crowd got larger, which made it virtually impossible to get a seat unless you arrived early. We arranged karaoke night, and even had the group commander entertain us with his charming voice. It was great to see the young folks, especially, get up and dance. This did not make the time go by any faster; however, it helped to boost morale.

A Woman In the Midst of the War

From a woman's perspective, I am glad that I stepped up to the challenge. I volunteered for an out-of-cycle AEF. The people who were aware of this fact thought I was crazy. However, I wanted to experience what many of my troops had already experienced. I was looking for and found growth. The conditions were difficult and sometimes unbearable, yet they seemed to be the same for the men.

One factor that became apparent to me was the number of

women who were present. Yet no matter how many women had key positions, there was always a man making the final decision—even though it may have been a woman's idea. For example, I was the Group First Sergeant, with eight unit First Sergeants under me (all male). However, there was a Group Chief Master Sergeant in my charge. We also had a female Deputy Group Commander, but the Group Commander, of course, was a man. I have no complaints, though, because I am living proof of the progress that has been made and will continue. Have things changed? Yes—slowly, but surely. Our history books have proven this fact. During earlier wars, women were only deployed for entertainment, or as nurses and nuns. I, on the other hand, have made history. My story can go down in the history books as possibly the only female Group First Sergeant thus far.

Looking Toward the Future

I have a new-found respect for all of the men and women who have served in previous wars. I plan to continue my journey and do all within my power to help us all return home safely to our loved ones. I am proud of what I have accomplished, and I thank God for the opportunity to serve my country and make my family proud. Fortunately, growing up in Trinidad more than adequately prepared me for my mission in Iraq. For those who do not understand or respect their freedoms in the United States of America, I challenge them to get off the sofa, stop watching the war on the television, and experience it up close and personal. As for myself, I am looking forward to a safe journey home, a hot bath, a full body massage, five days of continuous eating and sleeping simultaneously, lots of hugs, kisses, and laughter from family and friends, and praying that all the studying pays off and I make chief.

"I am searching for a different way to say—news is sparse. But, I won't change my basic belief—no news is good news because bad news travels fast."

First Sergeant Heather Williams' campsite,
Baghdad, Iraq, 2004.
"My story may go down in the history books as possibly the only female Group First Sergeant thus far."

"Lord, hold our troops in your loving hands. Protect them as they protect us. Bless them and their families for the selfless acts they perform for us in our time of need. Amen."

I Will Never Forget

By Pamela A. Morris

U.S. Air Force Staff Sergeant Pamela A. Morris was deployed to Tallil Air Base Iraq, from July to November, 2003. Originally from Collingswood, New Jersey, she is currently stationed in the United Kingdom as a postal specialist. She is the single mother of Shawna Souza, 8, and K. Andrew Souza, 7.

I will never forget the morning I left for Iraq. The weeks before my departure had been pretty difficult—preparing for this deployment was very hard. In early June, I was notified that I would leave the 28th of July.

As things turned out, I actually left the first week of July. I had deployed before, and things went smoothly, but this was different from the start. I had been in Saudi Arabia only a year and a half before, and had been at my new base for only six months when I found out that I would be leaving again. One of the reasons that I chose to come to this base was that people did not deploy from here. I am a single mother of two wonderful and understanding children, but this was supposed to be our change. We came to a small base so I would not have to work weekends or holidays, and would not deploy. Well—what a surprise when I was notified. I then had the hard job of telling my two children, ages seven and eight, that I would be gone for our first summer in England.

We had to decide where my kids were going to stay while I was gone. Their dad is also in the Air Force, stationed in Japan, and was also supposed to deploy sometime during the time I would be gone. A friend here stepped up instantly and told me that she would watch the kids while I was gone. What a Godsend she turned out to be. Since my departure date got moved several times, I didn't get to spend the time I needed with the kids before I left. It was the Fourth of July weekend, and I had to leave Monday morning. We decided that it would be easiest to let the kids spend the night at my friend's house, since I needed to leave early the next morning.

Of course, I did not sleep a wink that night. The next morning, I walked quietly through the house, whispering my goodbyes to my babies as they lay asleep, and after a few final kisses I had to go. What a feeling to leave your children asleep in someone else's house for four and a half months.

After a short journey, I landed at Al Udeid Air Base, Qatar. The first thing I remember is how hot it was. I spent the months of June through September in Saudi Arabia, and I never remember it being this hot. After we changed out of our civilian clothes into our uniforms, off I went to Tallil Air Base Iraq. Flying into the country, you could see the oil fires still burning. When we landed at the base, the first thing I saw was a blown-up helicopter on the runway. Later I would see several wrecked trucks, cars, airplanes, and helicopters all over the base that could not be cleaned up because the area had not been swept for landmines. Iraq is an extremely hot and dirty place, with bugs and rodents everywhere. When I first got there, we did not have hot food, and the water from the shower was the temperature of the outside air: extremely hot in the summer and cold in the winter nights.

This hellhole became my home, and believe it or not, coming back to the real world and my family was a struggle for me. I often think about the guys and girls who are still there—would you believe me if I told you that I actually miss it? When you come back, people do not understand what you went through, and there is no magic that tells people you served in Iraq. You again become one of the crowd—although the experience will never be erased from my mind.

As the days go by I start to wonder, "Was it a big deal that I was there?" I am now back with my children, and that is a GREAT feeling. We took a trip to Disney World when I got back. I treasure every moment I have with them, because who knows when I may have to sneak kisses to them while they sleep in someone else's house again.

"One of the things I can safely say is that being a Mom of a soldier is Hell."

Sheree Newton's son, Josh, with seized Iraqi ammunition. "I can't believe I thought a combat engineer built bridges and mostly did contracting type work."

Tallil, Iraq, 2003.
"I never remember it being this hot."

A Small Sacrifice for Such a Large Reward

By Curlen M. Martinson

Captain Curlen M. Martinson is with the 332nd Expeditionary Medical Group, U.S Air Force, deployed to Tallil Air Base, Iraq. She has two beautiful children, a wonderful husband and a frisky puppy. She has been in the military for 15 years and has thoroughly enjoyed her time and commitment to her country.

During duty on the 11th of November, things were fairly quiet. I was ready to go to my tent and crash on my cot. After a nice hot breakfast, I did just that. I was asleep when a large *boom* woke me up. The earth shook, and my friend and I sat up and looked at each other. No alarms sounded! We figured it was the ordnance group setting off unexploded rounds. We decided to doze back to sleep, but shortly after this we were alerted and had to report to the hospital. Here we were briefed about the suicide bomb that had gone off at the Italian complex in An Nasiriyah.

I was then assigned to work at the "search and seizure" area and ensure that no further injuries occurred to the patients. The number of patients and multiple injuries seemed never-ending. An infant was on one of the last vehicles that came through. I took the infant in my arms and felt sure that I could help the baby. I was then told that I could not do anything for the little one because the baby had not survived the blast.

Many emotions passed through my mind. I was mad that someone would take the life of an innocent child who didn't even have a chance at life, but I was glad that the infant had not received debilitating injuries for life.

On November 20, 2003, after working the emergency room, we got a call and were told we needed to respond to a "local Iraqi child" who had been in an accident. This mission involved leaving the base perimeter, which was considered more dangerous. Any missions off-base were considered volunteer missions. As the ambulance exited the base, I thought to myself, "What am I doing?

I have two kids to go home to." As we pulled up to the scene, I realized that I could help this mother with her child, and felt relaxed with my decision. Once on the scene, I heard crying from several people. I saw an older adult in back of a truck and thought, "This isn't a child."

But then I saw the mother hitting herself in the face, and the father crouched over on the ground and pounding on the earth. We examined the young man to find no pulse, a bloody face, obvious bilateral broken wrist, and a broken neck. He was dead on arrival. The young man was 23 years old.

Looking around, I saw that no one had provided any comfort to the parents or friend who was on the scene. As I approached the mother, we kissed cheeks, I hugged her, and she sobbed in my arms. The mother then tried to explain that this was her only child. Finally, I knew why I was here. I sat holding her and looking into her eyes; I saw her pain and sorrow.

In the distance, I saw nothing but barren land, a war-torn countryside. A cart and donkey went by, and suddenly, I realized why our commander-in-chief had ordered us here. I also realized that this *was* a child, and this child belonged to this family that watched him fall from a three-story building. The family was trying to strip the building and sell the parts for their living income. It was heartbreaking—I realized how unfair life could be. Earlier that night, I had worked up an arm fracture on a 23-year-old American who received the injury playing football. He didn't have to loot a building to survive.

On December 24, I couldn't sleep and decided to walk over to the hospital. I had heard that a little boy had been hit by a Humvee and had been in surgery most of the day. Once at the intensive care unit, I saw the six-year-old local Iraqi boy lying helplessly on the hospital cot. He had survived an eight-hour surgery in one of the dustiest operating rooms that one could imagine. He had both legs broken, a possible head injury, a broken ulna and radius in his right arm, and problems with his spleen. His prognosis was promising.

The technician on duty started to explain that she was concerned about his blood pressure because it was dropping. We were concerned about postoperative bleeding and/or a head injury. We repeated his vital signs and informed the doctor of our concerns. We ended up providing bag-valve ventilation for the boy and stabilized him for transport. As we left the hospital and transported the little guy to the aircraft, he opened his eyes several times and looked around. We felt he would be all right and not have any long-term disabilities. Perhaps he would have a good future. Many questions were unanswered as to the cause of his accident. Did he run out in front of the vehicle? Was he pushed or thrown in front of the vehicle for compensation? Life here in Iraq is not valued as it is in America.

On December 26, a 15-year-old girl brought herself to the outside gates of the base. She was here only one day before, due to a sexual assault attempt by a taxi driver. She returned to our hospital because she was threatened with death by her family. She had dishonored her family and now had to save her own life. She was so afraid that when she came back to the outside gate, she spent the night outside, alone and cold, because she knew she couldn't return home. Honor killings are very common here when a family member has "dishonored" the family.

One week prior to my arrival here in Iraq, a 16-year-old was set afire by a family member because she had dishonored her family. She died a couple days later. The females do not get a chance for innocence. Even if they are raped, it is considered "bad-naming" the family. As a mother, nurse, and officer in the United States Air Force, it is not always easy understanding the whys and hows, but knowing you can help is what makes the difference. My stories have been about the children because this is where my heart is. This has been a demanding, stressful, but very rewarding duty. I consider it a small sacrifice for such a large reward.

Update

Sara stayed in our facility for over a month. We awaited word from our command whether she would gain amnesty and be able to enter the United States, be returned to her family, or go to a government agency or local orphanage. Sara had grown very fond of some of the staff, and the staff had become very close to her. Our unit was also concerned about security issues (for our unit and for her), as she had heard multiple stories and conversations from the staff, walked around base with an escort, and had learned a fair amount of the English language. We had introduced her to the American way of life, and she was sure to have difficulty with re-entry into her culture. She dressed American-style, watched our movies, and played all American CDs.

Sara expressed a desire to learn about Christianity and wanted a cross necklace. We were not allowed to share the word of Christ or speak of religious preference to her due to our General Order #1. Giving her a cross necklace was believed to put her at increased risk in the Iraqi culture. She had grown accustomed to our way of life.

Sara became manipulative, and the staff became split on what should happen. Her family was actually from a nearby town and was asking questions. The oldest brother knew where she was, and word came to Sara that he was out to kill her. Sara could not go to a local orphanage or the United States, as her parents were still alive. The government agency felt at risk, and if she left the agency on her own, she would certainly be put to death. She was not granted entry into the United States due to her age and her non-orphan status.

On February 7, 2004, we received word that there was a Commander's Call. Once everyone showed, our commander announced that Sara was being taken to the head sheik of her area. The head sheik had written a letter to her family saying that he would take the shame/dishonor and the family was cleared. The head sheik would take her in, and her brother and father signed a contract stating that if any harm came to Sara, they could lose their lives.

Our commander said he was allowed to do checks on Sara once a month to ensure her safety. As our rotation departs, we will never really know what happened to Sara.

And some thoughts....

Sara was a very sweet girl. She was very smart as well. She would have been happy in the States, just like a typical teenager. I hope her rebellion doesn't get her in trouble. She quickly learned to work the staff to her advantage and work staff against each other. I was split in the middle. I didn't want anything bad to happen to her, but she became very close to the interpreter, and he was willing to do whatever was necessary to get her back to the States. I felt he might put me in a position where I would get in trouble (trying to work a way to get her to the States and not through the appropriate channels). He stated he was willing to pay for her entire transfer if he could make it happen. He asked me what I would do if it was in my hands. This bothered me and scared me.

I took Sara to the tent city basketball games, bingo games, and even to our New Year's celebration.

Sara had injured her arm during the taxi incident when running away from home. It was only a bruise, but even three weeks out she wanted an ace-bandaged wrap and ice pack placed on it. One of our staff members sprained her ankle and was on crutches. She was close friends with Sara. Within two days Sara twisted her ankle and was also given crutches by a technician. On her trips to the shower, she stood and placed weight on both ankles without difficulty, but she received a lot of attention for this and it continued for quite some time. Her story became widespread throughout our base (another reason for security concerns) and even the locals. Some of the local workers yelled comments at her. We had believed that Sara had come from Baghdad, but she was actually from a nearby city.

I consider myself a Christian and wanted Sara to know of my God. I couldn't speak to her about it, but she saw me pray over my food and speak to other staff members about God. When she spoke of a cross necklace that she wanted, I showed her my necklace and explained how it was a gift from my parents before I departed for Iraq. I would have loved to give her the necklace, but knew it might be harmful to her. I prayed for Sara and hoped she would be granted entry into the United States.

Sara had made great friends in our unit, and some wanted to take her home, but again, our General Order prevented adoption, and again, she had parents. Sara told me that she was one of six children and the only female. She also said that her brothers were mean to her. I can't even imagine what Sara went through, knowing her sole support system for her whole life was out to kill her. She cried often and said she missed her mother. When she received word that her oldest brother knew of her whereabouts, she cried and went into hysterics.

About two and a half weeks before the Commander's Call, Sara was told that she had three options: (1) To go to the government agency (2) to go to the local police in An Nasiriyah, or (3) to be taken to the front gate and released on her own. I was angry that these were the choices a teenager had to face. She knew that if she went to the police or to the gate she was dead, and she felt very strongly about that. Our command was basically forcing her to go to Baghdad. I think the part that bothered me was that she couldn't be sent to the U.S. because she had living parents, but she could be left at a gate on her own. I felt this was wrong.

I pray for a better life for Sara, and hope that she will continue to work to get to the United States. I was saddened by these events, as I feel she went out on a limb, and we only added weight to that limb.

"We arrived at our destination two days later, close to midnight. It was dark, hot, and dusty. We were scared and didn't know what to expect."

Defense Officials Offer Advice to POWs' Families

By Kathleen T. Rhem, American Forces Press Service

WASHINGTON, March 31, 2003—Defense officials want to make families of prisoners of war aware that what they say may hurt their loved ones.

Statements made to the media containing personal information about prisoners of war could be used by enemy interrogators to make life harder for POWs, said Air Force Col. John Atkins, deputy commander, Joint Personnel Recovery Agency, Ft Belvoir, VA

—Courtesy American Forces Press Service

The Latest From Iraq

By Pearletta Beth Ullrich

Pearlette Beth Ullrich is the First Sergeant of the 332nd Expeditionary Logistics Readiness Squadron. She is deployed to Tallil Air Base, Iraq.

I am the First Sergeant of the 332nd Expeditionary Logistics Readiness Squadron, which consists of more than 160 people. Most of them are U.S. Air Force, but I also have Estonian Air Force and Lithuanian Air Force troops in my unit. Our mission is to fuel airplanes/generators/vehicles; manage inbound/outbound flights; store jet/diesel/mo-gas fuels; palletize and load/unload cargo/passengers; repair vehicles, such as hummers/dump trucks/jeeps/fire trucks/medic vehicles/armored vehicles/fuel trucks/flat beds; plan all logistics for deployments and redeployments; and order and warehouse supplies/equipment/parts for people, aircraft, and vehicles. The supplies for people are usually things like coats, uniforms, and boots. My own boots will probably not last this tour, even though they were brand new when I left. I am very proud of my team—they are sacrificing so much to be here. I work with a great group of people.

Driving here is interesting, especially after a rain. Think of mixing flour and water or talcum powder and water… it's clumpy and worse than clay. I have my own vehicle. At first, I kept getting lost, but I knew that if I saw a checkpoint ahead, I had gone too far. But the worst part of driving is the huge speed bumps and the speed dips, which are more like craters. No, we did not make them to keep the speed limit down; it's just the war-torn land. When it rains here, it doesn't soak into the ground—it just stays on the surface. When Civil Engineering dug a trench to drain the water away from our tents, the water had only soaked a mere three inches into the ground. It was like having shallow lakes everywhere. After the rain, I was so excited to find out that my boots are waterproof—okay, maybe I have already been here too long.

This base, at one time, had the Tigris River running through the area, and it was a very rich land area for farming. The farmers who lived here and cultivated crops—mostly rice — were known as the Sunnis. Well, the Sunnis supported the U.S. during the Gulf War. This, naturally, did not sit well with Saddam, so Saddam diverted the Tigris River, which ended their water supply. The crops died and the ground became a dry riverbed. The Sunnis scattered to other places, and Saddam established an Iraqi air base here. We bombed it pretty badly during Desert Storm. You can still see the damage and pieces of MIGs, etc., lying about. It was in the "no fly" zone, so not much has gone on here since Desert Storm except that several countries' armed forces, including ours, created a base here at the beginning of Operation Iraqi Freedom. So… that's work at the air base!

My space in my tent is about 6' x 5', which is fine, since I only read, dress, and sleep there. There are eight women in the tent, including myself. Since our bases were being closed in Kuwait and Saudi Arabia, the Army convoyed material from those bases here and we were able to get what we refer to as "Cadillac" showers and bathrooms. Cadillac showers and bathrooms are like single-wide trailer houses with nothing but showers or bathrooms inside. Our water plant produces around 90K gallons of water a day. That isn't quite enough for the number of people we have here, so water rationing is in effect and we take combat showers. That means: turn water on, get wet, turn water off, lather up, turn water on, rinse, turn water off. The water must not be on for more than three minutes, but we are glad to have real American showers and bathrooms. We have HVACs hooked up to the tents to provide heat or A/C as well as ventilation. They run all the time, since the tents do not seal in heat or cold air.

We have a gym in clamshells (tents with hardened brace structures), with a floor made from heavy metal slats that are used to make temporary runways. We call the gym "Muscle Beach." We also have a church in a clamshell, named "Oasis of Peace Chapel." They even got a piano from the Kuwaiti base, and with the melting pot of military personnel here we have lots of talented people, so we have people playing guitars (people brought theirs from home) and the piano.

Our communications squadron did all the wiring and hookup for us to have phones. I now look at phones as a luxury item, along with a few other things that I had taken for granted. CE did all the electrical stuff, so we have lights. We have several tents put together for our chow hall and they are now serving four hot meals a day, the fourth being for night shifters. Its name is "The Tallil Tavern." They serve lobster and steak at least once a week. It's really good. All of our food comes from Europe—we do not eat anything that comes from this country. Since there are *two* ways to motivate people in a contingency environment—feed them well and tell them when they are going home—we are eating very well. They overcook all meat, but it's still good. Other highlights are a movie theater, pool tables, morale phones, morale computers, and a juice bar in a bunch of tents put together, called "Hot Spot." We also have a library in a tent known as "Chill Spot." We have volleyball courts and a basketball hoop, plus washers and dryers in a tent, which beats hand washing in a bucket any day. We have it really good; of course it hasn't always been this way. So… that's living!

Life in a combat zone requires that everyone be vigilant on issues of force protection and safety. We (leadership) constantly remind everyone that we are in a combat zone and must all stay vigilant of our surroundings. If something or someone seems out of place, it probably is, and we want to ensure that everyone reports anything out of the ordinary. We all have to carry IPE (Individual Protective Equipment), such as helmet, flak vest, etc., with us at all times. If we hear the siren or "Alarm Red," it is not a drill. Take cover! There are no exercises here. We are not having an Operational Readiness Inspection by higher headquarters.

Safety is another priority. It's hard to see at night or during dusty winds, which are dangerous for those on foot, so Air Force personnel cannot walk outside of the compound (compound is same as tent city, which is on the base). No driving is allowed in the compound unless you are repairing water pipes, electricity, refueling generators, etc.

Another major safety concern is UXOs (Unexploded Ordnances). They are everywhere. Of course, they were a result of our activities during the Gulf War, Operation Desert Storm/Kuwaiti Liberation, and the initial bombing for Operation Iraqi Freedom. Cleared areas are marked, and no one may walk or drive outside of those areas for any reason. One of our CE folks recently found some fresh tire tracks in the mud with a live submunition in the tire print. Someone got very lucky. What do we do when we find UXOs? Our EOD (Explosive Ordinance Disposal) Team or the Italian EOD Team safely explodes them. We have some very beautiful, smart, and well-trained explosive-seeking dogs that check all postal mail, packages, or other containers that might conceal explosives.

This base has many damaged or destroyed buildings, aircraft, trucks, etc., from the war. We work out of some of the buildings, which are all made of cement. CE put in lights and COMM installed phones and land lines, but no running water. We have portable potties for the buildings we work in. We ship in bottled water for drinking. Life here is quite different from free America. However, we still have it far better than the Iraqi people. So, that is how it is, living in a combat zone.

The Coalition Forces working with the Air Force are Italian, Estonian, Lithuanian, British, Dutch, and Korean air forces. The Coalition Forces working with the Army are Romanian, Italian, and Korean armies. It is amazing all the good that stuff we, as a team, have done in Iraq. Of course, I'm sure that news hasn't made it there, since it's not bad stuff. Here's some of what the American news media won't tell you.

The Coalition has cleared over 14,000 kilometers of weeds out of canals, so now they can irrigate tens of thousands of farms. Thc first battalion of the new Iraqi Army has graduated and is on active duty; therefore, over 60,000 Iraqis now provide security to their citizens for the first time in 35 years. The Shiites recently celebrated the pilgrimage of the 12th Imam (I don't know what the 12th Imam is, but it sure is important to the Shiites). Iraq has a single, unified currency for the first time in 15 years. (We fly Saddam's money out of here to be destroyed after it is replaced.) Pharmaceutical distribution has gone from essentially nothing to 12,000 tons, and we have helped administer over 22 million vaccinations to Iraq's children. We built shelves for the orphanage's schoolhouse—and get this, satellite dishes are now legal. We got Saddam—everyone is free to come and go—no more citizens are imprisoned or murdered because their parents disagree with the government, and political opponents aren't imprisoned, tortured, executed, maimed, or forced to watch their families die for disagreeing with Saddam. *We got Saddam—Iraq is free!*

I believe that what we are doing is a good thing. The Iraqi people cheered, danced, yelled, screamed, and shot guns in the air (we weren't too crazy about that), when the news came that "We got Saddam!" Saddam's first words were, "Can we negotiate or talk about this?" The platoon leader replied, "Yes, President Bush sends his regards."

The Christmas Eve service last night at the Oasis of Peace Chapel was marvelous. Abraham was born six miles from here. Not many can say that they spent Christmas where Abraham once walked. In this time of reflection, Christmas has taken on a whole different feeling. There are no Christmas trees on every corner and in every house, no decorated yards, no families to visit, no visiting families, no football, no great meals, no malls, no stores, no sales, no gifts to wrap, no last-minute shopping, no credit cards, no eggnog, no beer, no wine, no hustle and bustle, no crowds, no looking for parking.... I could go on and on. So when that stuff is absent and the family is our comrades, then there is only one thing left on our minds and in our hearts—Jesus. *Now, that is Christmas!*

The latest from Iraq!!!

I am still doing fine ... exercising at the gym ... working ... sleeping ... reading ... and of course, doing crossword puzzles! I hope everyone is well.

Here's what has been happening in my neck of the desert. About work: as a First Sergeant, I have not had a day off since I put the uniform on at Qatar. However, I do have time to relax. It rained yesterday, and my boots leaked. As you may recall how happy I was to find out that they were waterproof, well, not so when you have worn them out. So, I will be getting a new pair of boots. It has been cold here, so with wet feet and socks, my toes felt like they were frozen. I don't get lost anymore, but the speed craters are getting deeper. I am always going everywhere on this base since my troops are so spread out, and there is a lot of walking. The morale here is so high … higher than stateside, or any other place I have been. Now that doesn't mean that they would not catch an aircraft home immediately if given the go-ahead. It just means that we are stuck as a family for a while, so we make the best of it. The duty is harder at Carswell than it is over here, because here, we are really doing what we're *always* training to do.

What a life. We had a New Year's Eve party. It started with a talent show, then music. I even had a date. I wore civilian clothes for the first time since I arrived. It felt strange. I only have the pants and top that I wore when I left. The pants are now too big. I read on a chart that the ideal weight for a female my age and height is 127 pounds; three more and I am there.

Oh, back to the New Year's Eve party. Champagne was grape or apple sparkling non-alcoholic wine. I like apple juice, but that stuff was nasty. The grape was okay. I tried non-alcoholic beer for the first time in my life. It's not good. Oh, yes the date. Well, he works in CE, and we flew over on the same rotator (rotator is a chartered civilian aircraft/company) and military aircraft, and we have been hanging out. Sometimes he treats for lunch….Uh, okay, the chow hall, and it's free … cheap date. Anyway, don't get any ideas, we are just buddies, someone to talk and joke with to make the off time fly, like the work time. Okay, I think he fancies me … and I, ditto. Well, I have been here for 45 days, and I am still happy and smiling all the time. My troops think I should seek mental health treatment. But, overall, I think they like me around because of the outstanding positive attitude that I have. It's contagious and besides, it could be worse, a lot worse. Remember the *two* ways to motivate people in a contingency environment (feed them well and tell them when they are going home). The variety of food is starting to look and taste the same every day. We are still eating very well, but the salad bar is basically non-existent. When I return to America, I will probably never eat rice or Brussels sprouts again. We have them almost every day.

The "Tallil Tavern" closed, so now we are being 100 percent fed by the Army. They actually do a very good job. We have TCNs (Third Country Nationals) contracted for laundry. They are searched, escorted, and guarded from the time they enter the base until they depart the base. I do not wash anything; everything goes to the contract laundry, which is inside the compound. And get this … it's free!!!! Oh yes, life is getting better.

About being in a Combat Zone: I really love this unit that I am assigned to, as they are such a great group of people. I am very proud of my team, but they do cause concern sometimes. A couple of days ago, I spent the evening in ER with one of my guys who lost a finger. The doctor explained to me what was happening and what the surgery would consist of. The surgery took about an hour. Okay, that was the first time I had really observed what, where, and how our medical folks do things in a combat zone. They do have the cleanest tents. I spoke with my troop as they rolled him out of OR. The nurse said he would not be able to recognize me or talk to me. I patted him on the shoulder and said, "Hello, Bobby, I'll be there when they get you settled in."

He never looked at me, but he said, "That's my First Shirt." The nurse was wrong on that call. The doctor briefed me, I visited for quite a bit, then picked him up when they dismissed him and drove him to his tent (okay, the hospital tents are only about a ten-minute walk to the farthest tent, but Bobby was a bit drugged). You know how the civilian medical folks always converse with the immediate family? Well, in a combat zone, that happens to be the First Sergeant, which is me.

I love being a First Shirt!!! I am the right hand for the commander, and I get to know everyone on the team. Some of my team went on an Army convoy. They had been gone many hours when I got the news they had been attacked. I was pacing a bit on that one until I found that no one was injured. I don't think one of the trucks survived, but that's nothing to us. Being a First Sergeant can be hard. You need to accomplish the mission, keep everyone safe, healthy, happy, and above all—*focused.*

The EOD team is still blowing up UXOs—unexploded ordinance—bombs. That has become a daily event. Another part of my job is to improve the quality of life for my team (TVs, DVDs, mattresses in tents, etc). Aren't we spoiled with the comforts of home? We do have to be careful. Two rows of Army tents burned to the ground because of overloading circuits. So guess what, we have fire safety inspections of all tents by our fire chief. With UXOs, tent issues, driving hazards, walking hazards, etc., we really work hard *not* to do the enemy's work for them.

U.S. Air Force personnel are not allowed to possess, purchase, or consume alcohol over here (General Order #1). They have found ways, which doesn't surprise me, and I am having meetings with the troops to reiterate the order. If caught, it's a violation of Article 92, punishable by up to two years in prison and a dishonorable discharge. We are serious. The real reason for that order is that we must stay focused and vigilant. And I really want to know that the people that I am working with are alert. Plus the alcohol over here is not regulated, so they could be drinking gasoline.

War.... Combat Zone.... It's not what it used to be. Before, we knew who the enemy was. They were in uniforms and charging or flying toward us. Today, they are terrorists without uniforms, and could be that elderly person in a wooden cart being pulled by a donkey, and that cart just happens to be loaded with bombs. No joke—that happened. Every car, every person, is a potential weapon. We can't trust anything. We continue to maintain a high state of vigilance against an enemy that can be anybody who just waits and probes for weaknesses. We did expect more activity after we got Saddam, but it actually went down. I suspect that some of his supporters no longer felt threatened that he would come back.

I still believe that what we are doing is a good thing for the people of Iraq. I guess you heard about the U.S. Navy seizing more than 200 pounds of heroin and methamphetamines, as well as confiscating nearly two tons of hashish. They believe it to be tied to Osama bin Laden's terrorist network and the first of Al Qaeda links to drug smuggling. *We got Saddam—now we must get Osama bin Laden!*

I went to Ziggurat on New Year's Day, which was an amazing trip. We cannot build anything today that will last 20 years; however, a lot of Abraham's house is still there from 4000 BC. Everyone was in awe of the entire area.

Well, it is 2004. Happy New Year!!! It is a new year with new challenges, new adventures, new goals, and best of all, I'll be back from Iraq!!!!

4th ID soldier in armored personnel carrier with man's best friend

And It Begins

By Amy Hansen

U.S. Air Force 1st Lieutenant Amy Hansen is with the 3rd Wing Public Affairs Office, Elmendorf Air Force Base, Alaska. She was commissioned out of the Reserve Officer Training Corps at the University of New Hampshire in December 2000, and served at Langley and Columbus Air Force Bases before moving to Alaska. She would like to dedicate this story to her parents, Brian and Janet Hansen, for inspiring her love of reading and writing.

It was a nice day—a clear day, slightly chilly for Virginia in the fall, with a sky painted watercolor blue.

Through the propped-open door, I could see maintainers, mostly 17-to-18-year-olds, milling around in the common room. Some were busy with thick binders of aircraft forms, while others were bragging to their buddies about their latest Saturday night conquest. Almost all had paper cups of coffee in hand to chase away the early-morning chill.

Lost in my silent observation, I felt, rather than saw, Senior Master Sergeant Thomas push himself away from the navy blue "six-pack" work truck he had been leaning against while he chatted with another supervisor. I could feel him because his very motion stirred the air—a large, dark man with a broad head whose intimidating stature contrasted with his quiet voice and quick laughter.

"Senior" Thomas meandered over a stretch of asphalt to the picnic table where I sat, enjoying the fresh air and watching the early-morning movement on the flightline. The F-15 Eagles were lined up in perfect rows—muted gray metal triangles with three stubby legs for the landing gear wheels, sitting silently, lethally, on a field of dull brown cement.

Soon the maintainers, clad in navy blue coveralls and carrying toolboxes, would file out of the break room. Shortly after that a few of the jets would begin to emit their signature high-pitched whines.

Even now on the quiet flightline, the smell of the Air Force was unmistakable: the sharp, intense, oily, ever-present gasoline smell of JP-8 jet fuel.

My first encounter with the pungent smell of JP-8 was during Field Training at Tyndall Air Force Base, Florida, where they train F-15 pilots. As a Reserve Officer Training Corps cadet at the University of New Hampshire, I had been taking classes each semester, learning about the Air Force without ever having set foot on an actual Air Force base. In fact, I had even agreed to serve four years as an officer upon my college graduation. In return, my tuition, room, and board, amounting to over $25,000 a year, would be paid for by the government. When I signed the papers agreeing to the scholarship money, my only experience with the military was two ROTC classes a week during my freshman year.

I was fortunate. I enjoyed my experiences learning to march (or drill, as we called it). I liked the camaraderie of high-caliber people working toward the same goal. And although I hated wearing a uniform once a week around campus, it did make me feel distinguished and important.

Field Training, however: a four-week course of intense physical training and mental challenges between my sophomore and junior year of college, reminded me of my priorities. As F-15s thundered above chasing unmanned drones and shooting them down with live missiles, the 100-something degree weather, the harsh military training instructors, and the impersonal environment of "boot camp" forced me to examine the realities I would face as an air force officer.

Scholarship or not, I always wanted to serve in the military. An avid reader, I was fascinated by tales of the Revolutionary War—of the weak American colonies uniting and conquering the great British empire on the strength of their convictions about freedom and equality. But when my Field Training Officer discussed the clause in the commissioning oath about defending the Constitution of the United States of America, he encouraged us to think about whether we could deal with the reality of upholding that oath.

Could I kill someone? Could I watch one of my friends be killed?

Could I handle leaving my family behind if I was killed? Could I do this all on the strength of my convictions about the importance of freedom? My father, who had served briefly in the Army during Vietnam, had asked me the same questions. With the smell of JP-8 pricking my nostrils, I made the decision during Field Training at Tyndall Air Force Base that the ideology that founded this country was one that would far outlast my short life. I would die for it.

Two and a half years later, now a second lieutenant stationed at Langley Air Force Base in Hampton Roads, Virginia, I watched Senior Thomas walk toward me and I rose from the picnic table to meet him. He showed me the 27th Fighter Squadron's flying schedule for the day and pointed out the tail numbers of the F-15s that would have to be "generated," or made ready, for flight that morning.

I tugged on my Battle Dress Uniform, or BDU shirt, the top of the green camouflage uniform that most people associate with the Army. The one-size-fits-all-genders philosophy in the military never seemed to accommodate my womanly rear end. The flight suit, which I had been wearing for most of my six months on active duty, was even less flattering to anyone with more-than-generous curves like my own.

I had switched uniforms so as not to stand out in the maintenance section of the squadron, where I was observing and learning this week. Despite my best efforts to blend in, many of the troops still considered me an outsider because of my status as a pilot training candidate. I was learning the ropes in the 27th Fighter Squadron before beginning pilot training in Columbus, Mississippi. My big move was now less than three weeks away, at the end of September.

Senior Thomas, though, never treated me with anything but respect, regardless of my transient status, and I genuinely looked up to and learned a lot from him. As he pointed out the problems his troops would face today—a shortage of supplies, an unidentified electrical malfunction, a foreign object lost in a cockpit—I admired the grit of this senior non-commissioned officer. Daily, he inspired hundreds of young men and women to keep an aging fleet of jets flying safely for often ungrateful pilots and supervisors.

When we finished with the forms, Senior Thomas told me to check out headphone-like hearing protection so that we could go out on the "line" safely. While I walked over to the supply counter, its double doors propped open to the fall morning air, he disappeared into the common room and then into his adjoining office.

Moments later, he returned to the doorway and motioned me over. I joined a group of about three others in Senior Thomas' tiny office, huddled around a radio. Confusion, denial, and disbelief skipped across their faces as reports of a commercial airliner crashing into New York's World Trade Center were outlined in sketchy eyewitness reports. It was September 11, 2001.

When the second airliner hit the World Trade Center, most of the supervisors in the squadron were watching it on television. What could have been explained away as a terrible mistake was no longer an isolated incident. One at a time, we wearily stood up from our chairs to man our duty stations, ready to begin our fight against an unknown enemy. I knew that for the duration of the crisis I would have to go back to the operations section of the squadron, where my fighter scheduling experience was needed the most, so I stepped outside to tell Senior Thomas.

I blinked away the sun and looked up into the painted sky. Two gray triangles were dotted against the serene blue in the distance. They roared toward me, high above, with a distinctive engine whine. The jets, our jets, would arrive over the Pentagon in less than an hour. The smell of JP-8 tickled my nose, and I smiled as I turned and went in to work a long string of 12, 14, 18-hour shifts.

In my own small way, I was fighting back.

"I thank God for the opportunity to serve my country and make my family proud."

Camp Cold Steel, outside Tikrit, Iraq April 26, 2003.
"Our country should always remember that many of our finest men and women demonstrated immense courage in making the ultimate sacrifice for their country."

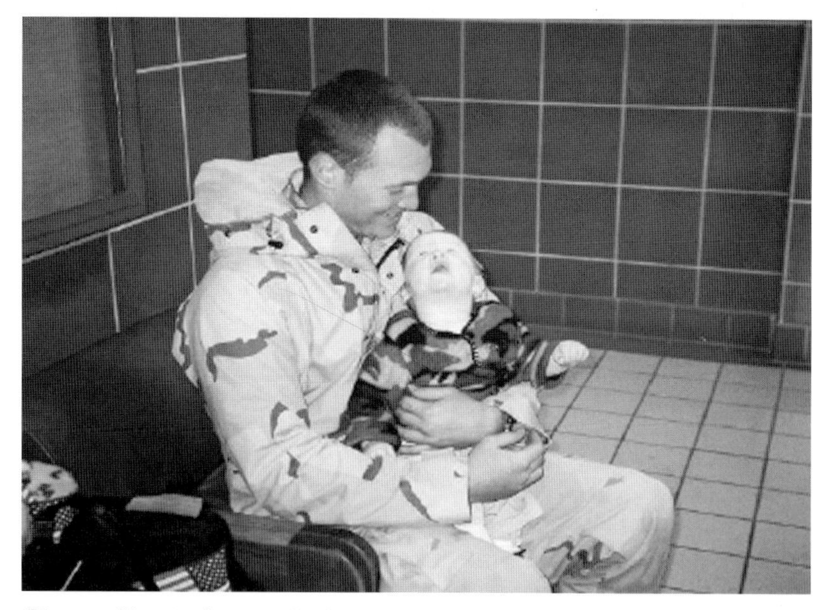

Sheree Newton's son Josh playing with his son Hayden, who was born while he was in Iraq. Sheree writes, "As I sit here tonight watching my grandson sleep, I see his father and I smile."

Renate ‘Rain’ Nietzold’s son, Shawn.

“We can’t put into words and do justice to what we feel inside, and what our thoughts are.”

Sheree Newton’s husband Craig, daughter-in-law Jeni, and grandson Hayden, welcoming her son, Josh, after almost a year in Iraq.
“I want to be the mother my son remembers when he gets home, and not a fragile wreck.”

Daughters

War casts a long shadow at a high school in Killeen

By Robert W. Gee, American-Statesman Staff, November 8, 2003

Killeen—At Robert M. Shoemaker High School, war echoes loudly. News from Iraq arrives by cell phone and e-mail; often before the cable news tells it in the counselor's office. It races through the hallways, from classroom to classroom, carried on the lips of students who live the war every day. The days when word comes of another attack, another death – that is almost every day – they pray that it isn't mom or dad.

One or more parents of at least 800 students – nearly 40 percent of the student body – are serving in Iraq or have orders to deploy early next year. About half of faculty members have spouses, children or brothers or sisters serving in Iraq.

—Reprinted with permission of The American-Statesman

The Missing Face

By Lindsey

Lindsey is the daughter of an Air Force Dental Corps colonel, who is deployed to Iraq.

I scanned the faces of proud parents, relatives, and friends in the growing audience, but the tassel from my hat kept obstructing my view. I knew there would be a face missing in this crowd—but I had to look for it anyway. My mom was the first to catch my eye, as I slowly began to recognize the tiny faces in the back of the auditorium. My own little fan club of grandparents, aunts, cousins, sisters, and close friends had come to witness and celebrate the closing of a large chapter in my life. My disappointment grew as the reality hit me—he had not been able to make it. Many times that year I had hoped his face would be there, but it was not—when I was crowned homecoming queen, when I hit my first triple, or even when I struck out to lose the big game. I knew that he was not just around the corner—he was halfway around the world.

The war—Operation Iraqi Freedom—had filled much of the news, as well as most of the discussion in our government class. But for me, the war had become much more than that. I took notice of the students surrounding me on stage. Each set of eyes was dancing with eagerness. The plans for our next chapter would begin to unfold after tonight. The options were endless. I marveled as I recognized the precious gift of freedom that we each had—the freedom to plan, to learn, to achieve. Those freedoms come at such a heavy price. My selfishness quickly became apparent to me as I realized the infinitely small price that I had to pay in order to claim such a precious gift as my own. I knew that there were many like my dad who, even at that moment, were sacrificing their very lives, so that I.... my thoughts were interrupted by the sudden hush of the audience. The principal stepped onto the platform where he welcomed the guests and introduced our class. Then the formalities—prayer, speeches, and special awards.

Finally, our names were called, one by one. I received my diploma with cheers from the crowd, a strong handshake, and a smile that went beyond the pleading eyes of the photographer. Although I wish that my father's face had been there at that moment, its absence had allowed me to experience, on an extremely small scale, the sacrifice that pays for my freedom.

"My son is so aggressive, I just don't know how to deal with his frustration and anger. He's so far away and I feel so helpless."

The recognized symbol for the loss of a soldier in combat reminds us that freedom isn't free.

War on TV Affects Students of Deployed Parents, Parents, Teachers
By Sgt. 1st Class Doug Sample, USA American Forces Press Service

WASHINGTON, March 31, 2003—Many children may not understand the principles and politics behind America's war with Iraq or the war on terrorism, but nonetheless they see images and hear news in the media.

The frightening images of war being brought daily to homes throughout America can be disturbing enough for adults, but they're even more so for children, especially those whose parents are deployed, said Joseph Tafoya, director of the Department of Defense Education Activity.

—Courtesy American Forces Press Service

Hope

By Brandi Martinez

Brandi Martinez is 17 years old and a junior in high school. She is stationed in England with her mom and step dad, who are both in the Air Force. Her step dad is deployed to Iraq.

Fear and excitement hang over this head,
wanting to fight and bring justice.
Fighting to protect loved ones present and future.
Knowing that while being gone,
birthdays and holidays will be missed.
Reassuring family of a safe return, as with a sad "Goodbye,"
home and family are left behind.
Torn from love and comfort and dropped into a country draped in a blanket of pain and sorrow, the scent of tortured souls fills the air.
As it sinks in that this is to be home,
and what is to be thought of as family, for months uncounted.
Each soldier protects the other, and hopes for the best.
Fear and excitement hang over this head.
Praying for God to bless the living and the dead.
Waiting and hoping to go home.
Knowing that if this life is lost, others will live on, that liberty is still ours, and that the pursuit of happiness will continue on.
Hope carries the soul of soldiers.

"God, I hate war... my heart goes out to everyone who will be forever affected by this horrible tragedy of war."

Girlfriends

Lori Burling

Daniela SantaMaria and boyfriend Tom

Jenny Dural

Maripaz Garcia and boyfriend Enrique

Girlfriends

U.S. troops stage massive operation for suspected militia leaders in Iraq
FALLUJAH, Iraq, 2003/6/16, Chris Tomlinson, AP

U.S. soldiers backed by helicopters and tanks raided homes, rounded up suspects and confiscated weapons in the restive town of Fallujah on Sunday, part of a nationwide campaign to root out anti-American insurgents who've been stepping up attacks. Operation Desert Scorpion, launched Sunday, involves a series of sweeps throughout Iraq using most of the U.S. Army units present in the country, said Army Capt. John Morgan, a spokesman for the Army's V Corps.

Three Generations

Lori Burling

Lori Burling's boyfriend, Jimmy, was deployed to Ali Al Salem Air Base in Kuwait, nine months before the war, and was part of it right from the beginning. Lori Burling, 26, is a former reporter for The Associated Press. After her boyfriend, 1st Lieutenant James Alves, U.S. Air Force, completed a year-long tour in Kuwait, the two moved to San Antonio, Texas. Lori is now an editor for the publications department at the University of Texas at San Antonio. Lieutenant Alves, 25, is a security forces instructor at Lackland Air Force Base. The two share a home with a black lab, Bella, and a cat, Hobbs.

My grandfather was in World War II. My father was in Vietnam. My boyfriend was in Operation Iraqi Freedom. Growing up, I can remember my grandmother and my mother saying things in passing about the wars, but nothing with any substance—or so I thought when I was younger. One thing that does stand out in my mind is that neither my grandfather nor my father talked about their parts in either war—a very different scenario from my boyfriend, 1st Lieutenant James Alves, security forces for the U.S. Air Force. At times, talk of the war consumed our relationship.

I met Jimmy in the summer of 2002, three months before he was scheduled to deploy for a year-long tour at Ali Al Salem Air Base in Kuwait. It was nearly nine months before President Bush attacked Iraq, but he was in the midst of talks indicating that the United States had every intention of defending our country from future terrorist attacks. While in Kuwait, Jimmy would be the Chief of Terrorism Force Protection and be in charge of protecting personnel at the base and installing safety measures to deter terrorist activity.

I have to admit that part of my initial attraction to Jimmy was that he was an officer in the Air Force. When I met him, he was stationed at Barksdale Air Force Base in Shreveport, Louisiana.

He was a Yankee, however—born and bred in Boston. I loved his accent, loved the cop talk, loved his knowledge of the impending war, and, of course, I loved the uniform.

At the time, I was working as a print journalist for an international company based in New York. My bureau was in Louisville, Kentucky, about two hours from where I grew up in western Kentucky. Following September 11, my bureau covered the military extensively. Kentucky is home to hundreds of brave soldiers—the 101st Airborne Division at Fort Campbell. You can imagine the amount of days I spent at the base. Regardless, as a journalist, I was a news junkie. I watched or read stories about the situation in the Middle East nearly eight hours a day. Hence, Jimmy intrigued me from the beginning; I met him through my aunt, whom I was visiting in Louisiana. Our first conversation zeroed in on September 11, and our first date was in a Humvee, touring Barksdale.

As our relationship grew stronger, the time we had together dwindled. We didn't talk about his deployment much at that time. We were too inquisitive about each other, staying on the phone for hours, talking about us, politics—anything but the situation in Iraq. We took a 12-day trip up the Northeast coast together, spent a week in Boston with his family, and he made several trips to Kentucky in between. In a way, I think I was excited that Jimmy was deploying—for him and me. He was going to play a part in history, and I was going to have this adventurous romance, just like my grandmother and mother had years ago.

My grandmother didn't talk much about the war, but she did talk about the correspondence between herself and my future grandfather. My grandmother has dozens of letters from when she and my grandfather wrote to one another. I never read them, but in my mind, they were relentlessly romantic. She would even dress up in costumes, including a bikini, and send photographs to him. My grandfather couldn't wait to get home, not even to propose. He sent a wedding proposal in a letter postmarked from Germany, along with money for my grandmother to purchase a diamond. The story has been embedded in my mind forever. To me, Jimmy leaving would simply be a chapter in our lives, hopefully one filled with romantic letters and adventurous tales.

He left the first day of November. He called from every airport—even from Portugal. He arrived in Kuwait safely, and he didn't waste time. He immediately started corresponding with me; however, it was through e-mails, not letters like my grandparents. I bet they were just as sweet, though. I did receive one letter from him while he was away. It came with Christmas goodies and a pair of his gloves. It read:

To My Lady,

The gloves are there so your hands don't get cold. They were mine, but I wanted you to have them, so I know your hands will always be warm because of me.

I love you,.

Your Lieutenant

It was the best gift I had ever received. However, unlike my grandparents, we discussed life after Kuwait rather than proposals and buying diamonds. With each conversation, I knew that Jimmy and I were meant to be together, and the happiness of knowing that consumed me. But at the same time, I was overwhelmed with fear. After Christmas, war talk was at its highest, and it started showing its ugly head in e-mails and phone conversations between Jimmy and me, and in every news story I read.

Then the phone call came—March 21.

"Babe, I don't have a lot of time right now because we all have to use the phone tonight. But I'm not going to be able to talk to you for a while. I'll try to e-mail. I love you."

Four hours later, President Bush told the nation that our military was attacking Iraq. Since meeting Jimmy, it was the scariest day of my life.

Thank God I was at work. I had a story to write, and it was my mission for it to be the best story of my life—for Jimmy, for the

101st Airborne Division who had already been deployed, and for all the other men and women serving our country. As I traveled the city hitting VFWs, college campuses holding prayer circles, and churches, I carried a lump in my throat. What was worse, every one of my friends called me in the first couple of hours following the initial attack. They all told me that Jimmy was in their hearts—their words swelled that lump.

I had to pull an all-nighter at work. I didn't mind, though, because at the office I could watch CNN, FOX, and MSNBC simultaneously. I couldn't close my eyes, and all I could think about was how I could make a difference if I were reporting from over there rather than Kentucky. Plus I might have an opportunity to see Jimmy.

Following my all-nighter, I went home at eight. I didn't go to sleep, though. Much to my roommate's dislike, I made up a cot in the living room and stalked the television, flipping among all the news stations while checking my e-mail every couple of hours, hoping for something from Jimmy.

After sleeping for a few hours I decided to take a shower, and it was there that the lump that I had been carrying around burst, and the tears swarmed me. I swear, more tears were swept down that drain than water. I didn't cry again until I received my first e-mail from Jimmy on March 24.

Hi Lady,

I love you so very much and I miss you tons. I am doing good, real tired, not getting much sleep as of late, but hopefully this will be over soon. It's funny, when I finally get relaxed, a missile alarm goes off and my heart starts going a million miles a minute, or I jump every time I hear a noise. I am going to have a lot of stories to tell you about this once I get home.

I love you.

Your Lieutenant

I kept myself busy with work for the next couple of weeks. I wanted to be a part of our stories regarding the war and the military around us. I spent a couple of days in Fort Campbell, writing about the soldiers who were deploying, most of them younger than I, still in their teens, packing guns that would eventually be used. I interviewed the soldiers' families, always telling them about my Jimmy, and how proud I was of him. I doubt they cared, but it made me feel better. Especially when I was talking to family members of fallen soldiers, and there were dozens. I knew in my head that Jimmy was safe, but it was still hard to believe that when writing about these men and women who had given their lives for me, my family, and my country.

It sounds like a cliché, but friends, family, and God got me through the days until I picked Jimmy up from the airport. I was dressed in red, white, and blue, carrying "Welcome Home" signs.

My friends are the ones who would drag me away from the computer and television on days that I felt the worst—what they referred to as the "dark days." They forced me to go to dinner or the movies to take my mind off Jimmy and the desert that was keeping him captive. It worked, too, and eventually I thanked them for their support. It was tough. I remember one night we were all playing pool at a hall near our apartment. One of Jimmy's favorite songs started playing on the jukebox—"Moon Dance" by Van Morrison—and I thought I was going to burst into tears in the middle of my shot. The gals took me home at that point. It was the small things that got to me. Jimmy and I had shared so many things in the short time we were together.

My mom was a trooper, too. She listened to me for hours crying about the hole that was in my life. When I went home to visit, she let me mope around. It was then that she shared more stories about my father's role in Vietnam. He was a paratrooper for the U.S. Army; stationed in Okinawa before his mission to Vietnam. My mom didn't meet my father until after Vietnam. He was shot in the leg and sent to Fort Campbell after arriving back in the States. Their war fears came afterward—my father's nightmares and his silence regarding the war. She's the one who told me that if I loved Jimmy, then he was the most important thing right now, "Do whatever you can to keep his spirits up while he's there and after he comes home." She was right, and together we came up with ideas for packages, cards, and his celebration once he returned.

I'm almost ashamed to say this, but God had never been a constant in my life. I knew the stories, I had been baptized, and I believed. But I never turned to Him for help—until March 21.

I prayed and prayed and prayed until I believed I had annoyed God enough to answer my prayers. I prayed for Jimmy's safety. I prayed for all of his pilot friends who were flying over Baghdad doing things that we civilians could never fathom. I prayed for all of the 101st Airborne soldiers and their families. I prayed for the attacks to end. But mostly I asked God to put Jimmy's fears on my shoulders so he could do his job. I realized that God was listening every time I heard Jimmy laugh on the phone, or he told me a joke in an e-mail. I knew God was helping him out, or at least showing me the path to make it easier for Jimmy.

In the end, Jimmy returned home safe and sound on October 29, 2003. He is different, but stronger in a way. He may not have been face-to-face with battle, but he was trained to do it, and he was ready. Hopefully, that is the closest he will ever come to harm while serving our country.

I think one of the toughest obstacles when Jimmy returned was that I had no idea what he went through in Kuwait and on his missions to Baghdad. As much as I watched the war unfold on my computer screen or television, I could never grasp what Jimmy had been through—the emotions that he had felt while lying in a bunker, protected by a gas mask and chem-gear during an "Alarm Red." I attempted to try to connect on some level, but then I gave up. I knew that as time passed, he would share more of his thoughts and fears from his time in the desert. And he did.

For me, it was an awakening. I finally realized why my grandmother would chuckle when I told her how romantic her relationship with my grandfather had been. There was romance for both of us, but there was also sadness and fear. War teaches you to appreciate what you have and to make the best of horrible situations. That's what my grandparents did, that's what my parents did, and that's what Jimmy and I did.

Jimmy has since been stationed at Lackland Air Force Base in San Antonio, Texas, teaching new officers about anti-terrorism. I joined him in November 2003, and I'm still working in journalism. I still have fears that Jimmy could be sent away at any moment, but at the same time, I know I can manage. Besides, Jimmy's job is to protect our country, and my job is to protect us.

"Tears on my pillow, pride in my heart."

Staff Sergeant Angela C. Rooney, Kuwait, 2003.
"They say wearing our uniforms will give us more protection if we're attacked by chemicals. So, we go to bed wearing some of the uniform."

4th ID soldiers in Kuwait waiting to enter Iraq, April, 2003. "You have endured the blazing sun. Having all the moisture sucked from your body. Being infested with sand flies. Eating out of cans or packages for months on end. Dealing with rats stealing your food."

U.S soldiers at Saddam Hussein International Airport, Iraq. "I don't let a moment go by without wishing our troops a safe return home."

Deployed troops return to thankful crowd

Associated Press, Wednesday, January 7, 2004. FORT CAMPBELL, Kentucky (AP)—Families of 101st Airborne Division soldiers waved American flags and yelled "thank you" as the division's first planeload of troops from Iraq stepped off the plane Wednesday after nearly a year at war.

.......Fifty-nine soldiers from Fort Campbell have been killed in the war — 57 of them from the 101st. The post has had more deaths in Iraq than any other military unit.

My Boyfriend

By Maripaz Garcia

Maripaz Garcia's boyfriend is deployed to Iraq from Fort Hood, Texas. Maripaz Garcia is a Ph.D. student in Foreign Language Education and a Spanish instructor at The University of Texas at Austin. She was born and raised in Madrid, Spain, and moved to the United States in 1993. In 2002, she met her boyfriend, Wilson Enrique Lopez, through a friend.

I don't care much about anonymity, and probably neither does my boyfriend Enrique, who is a soon-to-be sergeant at Fort Hood, Texas. We feel very much in love and wish to share positive feelings with anybody who wants to listen. We are tired of hearing sensationalist news and negative thoughts about war.

Yes, it is true that war brings poverty, death, and desolation. But we both believe that—apart from politics and media—some good conceptual and life changes will come out of all this devastation and destruction. Many people will eventually enjoy a better life—especially oppressed women—and opportunities to fulfill dreams will prevail over the difficult times. A lot of work is required, though—a lot of sacrifices on both sides, and a lot of understanding and hope. As a daughter of war and postwar survivors (Spanish Civil War), I think I have a distinct perspective of how the devastating effects of a war eventually weaken over time and the positive outcomes triumph, allowing freedom and opportunities to blossom and making the lives of future generations so much better than we ever dreamed possible.

That said, I would like to tell you about how my boyfriend Enrique and I stay afloat in our relationship. Nobody who has gone through this ordeal can deny that it is difficult to maintain a loving relationship during wartime. The relationship has to be strong to start with, and the couple must find ways to make it survive separation and conflicting feelings that will arise. If you have the determination to survive and the belief that eventually life will go on as well as it used to be, you can convince yourself that there is a way to overcome problems. You just have to work hard to find the way.

One of the ways that Enrique and I have discovered is humor. Our letters are filled with joy, hope, understanding, love, sadness, and patience, but also humor. A little dose of humor helps you cope with your stressful situation. It revitalizes your strength, it undermines the dangers of life, and, most importantly, it puts a smile on your—and his—face. We write each other as frequently as our jobs and life commitments allow. His letters are the sunniest part of my days, offering a little breath of tranquility and a sense of connection. Without this communication, I am not sure how we would avoid falling apart, getting distanced, forgetting about each other, and feeling abandoned. Once in a blue moon, we have the chance to communicate in real time (Internet or phone) and then reality hits you in the face, awakening you from that state of oblivion that letters can submerge you in. Yes, he REALLY exists, and he is just on the other side of the telephone line. You have been writing to a real person, not just an imaginary person in your head. There is nothing like real-time communication to shake you up a little and drag you down to earth.

Enrique, my boyfriend, is a very special person. I believe that only special people can actually survive a deployment, because it takes a lot of your strength and hope—which I didn't even know I had anymore. My boyfriend and I were together for only four months before his deployment. It is a short time to fall in love or make a decision about waiting for somebody for so long—and initially his deployment was only six months! We do have, though, a very special, strong connection that was pretty evident from the beginning. It is like something hits you in the face, and you finally open your eyes in anger to return the blow, when you realize that it was your own hand. It is a surprise, a wonderful feeling, and a sensation you don't want to lose. That is why, even with a short past and a long separation, I want to keep this relationship alive, give it a chance, and work hard on it. I believe in it. I am pretty sure he feels the same, and that helps me stay strong too.

Let me show you a sample of his letters. All of his letters are wonderful, and it was hard to choose one to show you how this relationship works. But eventually, I picked one that was emotionally charged and had a strong impact on me. When I attended the funeral of a friend's sister, I felt very depressed because it evoked in me painful memories of my own mother's death some years ago. That day, I missed Enrique immensely and wrote him a letter as soon as I got home. This is an excerpt of his letter back to me (translated into English):

Hello, beautiful girlfriend—

I hope you are a little bit calmer about all you told me on V's funeral. From the bottom of my heart, I want to tell you that even though it is true that I couldn't be with you that day, you have instead the certainty of knowing that you found somebody who will make his your melancholy and sadness, somebody who loves you with a very deep love, and who will always have a sincere and strong hug, so that you don't feel lonely. The kisses you needed that Sunday, the support, the love, the attention, and the warmth, you will have it all your life—if you want. I don't know if I can comfort you with words for all that great sorrow that you carry within yourself, but I would like to offer the warmth of an embrace and the gaze of somebody who knows how to listen with his eyes, his ears, his heart, and his soul. I want to take care of you and protect you, my little one, with all my love. In my arms, I will cover you with kisses and I will drink your teardrops.

The separation from this loving man is difficult, but at the same time we are still communicating, we are still strong, and wc are surer than ever before that our love will prevail. I hope to stay strong in the coming months, but mostly I hope to keep strong through the future downs of life. It is a question of overcoming difficulties with a strong determination, humor, understanding, patience, hope, and mainly, true love.

"The other day I attended X's funeral. I couldn't help noticing all the veterans in their uniforms. It was extremely emotional. It touched me deeply, when they saluted his flag-draped casket, as the pallbearers removed it from the hearse, and then most of all watching his father and mother, as they made their heavy way into the chapel. There was really no room anywhere, and there were a number of people from the media. I was trembling so much during Taps, thinking that my bones were turning to ice. So emotional, and so thankful that God had spared my son just one more day."

Homecoming banner Fort Hood, Texas, March 2004. "From a woman's perspective, I am glad that I stepped up to the challenge."

Jessica Howard's husband Gary, waiting to go back to Iraq after R&R. Little Gary is holding on to Daddy.
"Don't worry, I'll be home in December."

View from U.S vehicle driving through the streets of Iraq. "He said a female was driving, and the explosion blew her straight out of the left side."

That's Faith

By Amanda Knoll (Tucker)

Amanda Knoll lost and re-found her love because of Operation Iraqi Freedom.

There were no emotional goodbyes or one last kiss. I did not know the day or the time that he left. I did not know where his latest assignment had taken him. April 8, 2003 was the day he left for the war; April 8th was just another day for me.

I did remember the name of his unit, the 4th Infantry Division, 3/29 Field Artillery, which would have me scanning all news coverage for a hint of his whereabouts for the months to come. I dreamed about the conflict over there many nights, always seeing him in those dreams. With deployment orders in his pocket, my soldier and I went our separate ways in December of 2002.

The stress of Operation Iraqi Freedom proved to be fatal for our new-found love affair. Both right out of college, both scared of what the future would hold, we were still growing up as individuals. We called it quits; actually, I called it quits.

The strongest thing that he and I ever had in common was our faith in God. His faith, at the time, was much stronger than mine. Our families knew what a mistake our separation had been. We, on the other hand, were not so ready to admit it. One weekend that fall, ten months since we last talked, my soldier earned a couple days of R&R in Qatar (the Las Vegas of the Middle East). His father, who is one of his best friends, and a longtime supporter of our relationship, convinced the soldier to give me a call. His father then called me and convinced me to just be a good listener. I really was not sure how the call would go: what we would say, what we wouldn't say. We got to talk for about three hours that Friday afternoon, not so much about the war or the politics that used to keep us on the phone, but more about the life that we both were living without each other, and how much better even the worse things could have been if we had each other.

I think we talked again the next day three different times, a few hours each time. Those phone calls changed our lives, changed our directions, and restored my faith. Those phone calls made me prouder of him than I ever thought I could be of anyone. Those phone calls made me ache to see his face and hold his hand. Six thousand miles apart, we fell in love all over again with more honesty and intensity than the love we had known before. And that was the beginning of the relationship that everyone else who loves a soldier is accustomed to: the middle-of-the-night phone calls, the heart pounding to open the mailbox, and the thousandth prayer of the day said for the soldiers before marking another day off the countdown calendar. I wouldn't have wanted it any other way, though, because now I understand the phrase that happily married people use so often: "When you know, you just know."

Three hundred and sixty-three days after we had last seen each other, I picked Specialist Trenton Tucker up at the Colorado Springs Airport, and we had the moment that I think some people search for their entire lives: the moment when you know that no matter what you have to go through in life, or how difficult or wonderful it may be, it's better to go through it together than alone. This is the moment when your head realizes what your heart knew all along, that this is your soul mate. That night he came home from the war, Specialist Tucker asked me to be his wife, and for the first time in my life, I had no doubts or fears about answering with my heart. The most amazing things in life cannot be held or touched or even seen, for they are the things that you just feel so deep in your heart that you cannot explain. You just know. God gives you amazing peace, and you just know.

During his deployment, God let both of us go through some terribly difficult situations while apart from each other. From those situations we learned about who we are, who we wanted to be, and ultimately, that no matter how many months or miles were between us, God had a plan for us from the very beginning.

My feelings about the war are much different now than they were when my soldier first told me of his deployment orders. I have come to realize that there are worse things than war. Living in a world where there is nothing worth fighting for, or worth protecting, is by far more devastating than any war the world has known.

Those who love a soldier are better people for it, more humbled, more grateful, more proud, more patriotic and eventually, more patient. The women left behind may not secure the streets of Baghdad or patrol the banks of the Tigris, but the faith that the women of the war know is by far stronger than any fear that may seek out their loved one. How do I know this? Because when you know, you just know. That's faith.

"As our soldiers battle overseas, we have become fighters here on the home front."

4th ID soldier destroying Saddam Hussein portrait.

How Strong

By Daniela SantaMaria

Daniela SantaMaria's boyfriend was deployed to Iraq. Daniela SantaMaria is a member of Teach for America, through which she teaches first grade in Harlem, New York. She met her boyfriend, Tom, over soccer in South Korea, providing just enough time to fall completely in love before he deployed to Iraq's front line with the 82nd Airborne.

This brown-eyed girl was never supposed to know war.God knows I've tried to ignore it, bury it, or overpower it at least, with days and nights distracted by other adventures. But as long as Tom is fighting, war is my unwelcome obsession. We had talked about the war months before it happened, back in Korea where we met. It was just talk then, angry rambles at the newspaper I brought home every evening, sometimes with my own byline somewhere inside. I'd make a case for the "Just War" and other quaint Ivy League paradigms. He'd laugh at me, then explain how we simply did not have enough troops to pull off an operation like the one Washington suggested. Not that it mattered then. Within weeks I'd go back to finish school in New Jersey, and he'd stay right where I found him: a fond, camouflaged summer memory in the Far East. Any future war would just turn into a topic for a paper, frighteningly removed from my own experience. But then Tom received an invitation to come back stateside, and I fell in love. It didn't take much longer for this war to become personal.

I'm just a kid, really, young enough and green enough to think death is only for the old and jaded. Tom is neither, and so I kissed him goodbye at Fayetteville's bus depot nearly a year ago and began the countdown to his return. I've never really feared his death. I didn't even believe it in the dream I had last week, the one where the military knocked on my door with bad news. After all, he promised in one letter that he would not die out there, not now that he has a reason to come home. I've found plenty else to keep my mind racing after dark, though, mainly schemes to protect him from everything he has to see and do before coming back to me. But none of them have worked, and I've had to watch the world happen around me on the news and in the papers where this mess began. Every now and then, though, it hits me. *This is war. He can die.* I say those words again. *He can die.* It's a fact I only seem to realize when I'm alone, finishing up some work for the next day. It comes out of nowhere, really. I just roll over on my bed and start sobbing. It's as if I fight and fight and then finally, unexpectedly, I realize how tired I am, and I can't fight anymore. So I cry instead. The messy tears come for a good five minutes until I feel like a fool, wipe my eyes, and go back to what I was doing. I don't tell anyone and hardly recognize these lapses myself. I don't know how it would help if I did.

For now, though, on the surface, I look fine. I go to the gym wearing his old gym shorts at least twice a week and I haven't missed a day yet at my new job. Even my parents gave a visible sigh of relief the last time they saw me, noting that their little girl was doing all right. It's not that I don't miss Tom or talk about him. All of my first graders know about Miss S's soldier "friend." And I kind of enjoy provoking dropped jaws from strangers by casually excusing myself from a conversation to take a call from Baghdad. For the most part, though, I just try to overbook my planner, and tell myself the same thing I tell the confounded, apologetic eyes of my acquaintances. *This is not real. He cannot die.* And I'm okay for another day.

On those rare occasions, however, when my show is not convincing, my friends practically cheer my humanity. It's almost like they expect me to cry, and so they're better prepared for that reaction than the usual dry jokes I crack. They even call me strong when I cry. My roommate caught me in the act one night and said I'd handled Tom's deployment with fortitude and grace. This, as snot ran from my nose. I smiled, but I was more embarrassed than anything. This war has been perhaps the first time in my life that I've come to realize just how strong I am not. I've never wanted anything so badly as to bring Tom home. To bring him home safely. Home now. I've never felt so powerless to make something happen.

Whatever strength I do have has simply become a means of survival, anyway, in which case I don't want to be strong. I want to have this war and its implications end. I want to live again for today, instead of pulling through for tomorrow. I hate pretending that I don't mind having Tom gone, pretending that I understand and agree with the reasons that brought him to that hell, pretending that I condone the bureaucracy that will hold him in the Army for another two years while most of this country has the luxury to forget about guys like Tom. And I hate pretending that I can't comprehend his mortality just because I am 22 years old. All of this pretending takes so much energy, and I get tired, and then I stop believing my own charade.

When I lay these brown eyes on Tom again, I'll be one year less young, less green. There will be no denying that war and I have met, whether or not we should have. That's when it will all finally hit me. The fear, the anxiety, the desperately wanting him home and safe. I bet I'll cry before I even see him. I know the tears will come when I touch his face and listen to his stories under blankets and dark. I already wish this war never happened. I only hope that Tom and I will be able to look back eventually and know it did more than test our strength.

"I just did what I had to do, this wasn't a matter of agreeing or not."

Low number on leave list a precious gift

By Michael Hedges

Houston Chronicle, Oct. 25, 2003, 9:35 PM. TIKRIT, Iraq— Heat, fatigue and occasional danger have blurred the passage of time for many American troops more than six months into the U.S. occupation of Iraq. But soldiers unable to say if it's Tuesday or Saturday can usually recite one critical fact — their number on the leave list.

How I Found the Love of My Life

By Jenny Dural

Jenny Dural's deployed friend, Andrew Lutsch, became her boyfriend. Jenny Dural lives in Rochester Hills, Michigan, and is currently a sophomore at Michigan State University, with plans to attend the college of nursing. Private First Class Andrew Lutsch is in the 4th Infantry Division and was deployed to Iraq.

This story is about the love of my life, Private First Class Andrew Lutsch, who is in the 4th Infantry Division. I met Andy, my love, during my sophomore year of high school (he was a senior). We were together for about a year, and during that time, we fell deeply in love. Everything we did, we did together. He was my other half, and I his. But he was moving away to college, so he drifted away. We tried to rekindle our love a few times, but he was not ready. He broke my heart a few times during our spats of getting back together. He would tell me he loved me, and we would get back together, then he would decide he was not ready for us to be together after all.

One time when I went to see him at college, I gave him an ultimatum. This was his last time. If he broke my heart this time around, there would be no more tries. He did it again, as I knew that he would. After that, he tried so many times to get back together with me. It depressed him that I just wouldn't let him be with me anymore. I knew I loved him, but I did not want to get hurt anymore. He went through a lot during that time, and although we were not together as lovers, we were together as friends.

Andy decided to join the Army to make himself a better person. I knew that he was joining to run away from his problems (like me), and he needed an out from it, but I supported him. I knew it would help him through everything. During this time he always wrote me telling me that he loved me, and there was no other person for him. I loved him, too, but I was so afraid. He went to boot camp and right after that, he went straight to Fort Hood in Texas. He always told me (even before the war) that he had a feeling he was going to go to Iraq and that the United States was going to war. I never believed that would happen, because I just saw it as another attempt to get me back.

I remember the day that he told me he was leaving Texas to go to Iraq. It was during April of 2003 that he left. I thought, "Why is this happening? How can he leave me?" It was at that point I realized that he was the man for me, because I could not imagine my life without him. At the time I was with someone else, but we soon drifted apart because subconsciously, I stopped trying in our relationship.

During the summer of 2003, I fell back in love with Andy. It was weird, because I became his all over again while he was away in Iraq. I was his girlfriend again, and yet we had not kissed for about two years, and, he was a world away. Every day I would wait for the mail to see if he sent me a letter, and I would get so upset when there was nothing to read. The letters were a way to make me feel that he was still by my side. He was my strength through everything in my life, and I was his. I knew that no matter what I was going through at home, he had it much worse. Through our letters, I knew he was for real about us this time and he was finally ready for our love. I knew I was as well. I'd had relationships with other men in my life, but no one made me feel the way he did. I truly loved this man, and I knew that no matter what, I was going to wait for him to come home. The months went by, and every day it got harder to bear that he was in Iraq, and I could not protect him from harm. I cried a lot. I did not know what I would do if anything should happen to him, or worse, if he died.

I went back to college during the fall of 2003, and that was when our relationship really blossomed. His base eventually got Internet services so he was able to talk on Instant Messenger almost every night when not on duty. I put an alarm on my computer to notify me when he was online, usually around three or four o'clock in the morning. My poor roommate would be up all night hearing the keyboard going. We would talk for an hour or so, then he would have to go sleep or eat or maybe even go back on duty. It was the best thing the government could have given to the troops, next to coming home. I know it made Andy very happy and boosted his spirits. It was a way for us to feel connected.

The mid-tour leaves for the Army were also a blessing in Andy's life and mine. He was able to come home for two weeks in November of 2003. At first he thought he would not get the opportunity to do so because he had a low rank in the Army, but they picked him to go. I was so excited because at that time it was a year since I had seen him. And I was so anxious to be with him again. When he came home, it was so wonderful. Nothing in my life mattered but being with him. I spent the weekends alone with him, and it was like a fairy tale. It was better than our high school relationship.

Everything about our time together was perfect. I knew for sure then that he was the man I wanted to be with for the rest of my life, that he was my true love. His mother and family were so wonderful and kind to me, and my parents were also very supportive. They all knew of our past, and yet they still supported our love. I took him to the airport on November 19th to go back to Iraq. It was one of the hardest experiences that I ever had to endure in my entire life. His plane left at six o'clock in the morning on the 20th, so we stayed awake all night to make sure we didn't miss a moment together. At four o'clock we went down to the lobby and said our goodbyes. The last thing he said to me was, "I love you, Jenna, and I will see you in four months." I ran back up to the room in the hotel and cried for a few hours. Although I was completely worn down, I could not sleep.

As of now, Andy is back in Iraq and can only go online a few times a week, but I know that is more than most who are stationed there, so we are lucky. It really scares me now that something might happen to the man that I'm in love with. Unless they have experienced a similar situation, no one can know how it feels not knowing if they will ever see their loved one again. Not knowing if that last glance you took into each other's eyes will be your last. Not knowing if that last hug, kiss, or touch will be the last. It is a pain that no one should have to feel. I know that Andy is doing his duty as an American to protect his country, and for that I am so proud of him. He will always be the love of my life, and if something were to happen to him, at least I would know that at least once in my life, I felt true love. I pray to God every day that he will come home to me, and I thank Him for letting me receive the most precious gift of all: to love and be loved.

"Stay Smart! Stay Safe!"

Charlene Sawyer's son, Eric. Iraq, 2003.
"Shouldn't their attention be to keep their mental status as positive as possible so they remain alert to the danger they are facing?"

Sisters

War's 'end' a fallacy Military families fight fear each day

By Charlie Brennan, Rocky Mountain News, June 7, 2003

The war is not over. Not for the husbands, wives and children of soldiers still in Iraq. Only when those fighters again touch American soil and walk through their loved ones' front doors will the war be at an end for the ones left behind.

Eight soldiers with Fort Carson ties have been killed since May 1 - the day President Bush made a dramatic landing on the USS Abraham Lincoln, where he announced that "major combat operations in Iraq have ended."

—Reprinted with permission of the Rocky Mountain News

Family Members Left Behind: POWs of a Different Sort

(Just) One (of Many) Sister's Tale

By Serenity Rose King

Serenity Rose King's brother, a Sergeant from Delta Battery, Wichita Falls, TX, is deployed to Iraq. Serenity Rose King, and her girlfriend, Traci Phipps, live in the Dallas area. She grew up in a small Texas Panhandle town. She is applying for Graduate School, and she hopes to begin a career in Marketing/Public Relations soon.

Numbing. That's the one word I can come up with for what it's like to have a relative overseas right now. People occasionally ask me what it's been like to have Devin over there in a war zone. The truth of the matter is, I don't know what it's been like. I don't know where these past several months have gone. I don't even know what Devin looks like anymore.

I don't know how to explain to people that Devin has never been "just" my brother. He has been my best friend since the very first time I could talk, and he was my hero way before he became Sergeant Devin King, Delta Battery. I do know that no matter how prepared you think you are for something, it still can hit you pretty hard when it actually happens.

For several weeks before Devin was activated, I froze every time the phone rang. I would think "This is it," but it never was. Not until I was busy making supper one night, crashing around the pots and pans, dropping the package of burrito seasoning on the floor when the phone rang, *not* thinking "This is it"—not thinking anything, really. Then I heard Devin's voice at the other end. My heart dropped, an immediate lump formed in my throat, and I thought I was going to faint. Every word of encouragement muted in my head. Every prayer of hope turned to fearful plea. Every ounce of pride momentarily washed away with tears. Welcome to Day One.

And that's my new life: counting days, holding my breath, tossing through sleepless nights, and going through the motions during the long days. Welcome to a cycle of wishing, hoping, loving, waiting, hating, crying, wishing, hoping, loving, waiting, and so on. Some days I am optimistic, whereas other days I drown in the pity pool. Some days I laugh harder; some days I cry harder; every day I pray and wait. At first, I would start crying at the most random times: in my sleep, while I was brushing my teeth, while I was standing at the fax machine, while I was in line at the fast food restaurant, and the list goes on. I have gotten better about that … for the most part. Some days are harder than others, and some days are even harder than the hard days.

It isn't all pity parties and worry, though. Knowing that my brother is one of America's heroes is truly something to be proud of and appreciated for the dignified honor that it is. The thing is, though, Devin was my hero way before I had ever heard of Saddam Hussein. He has been a military man since the womb. In fact, to this very day, each of my parents still comes across one of his thousands of plastic green army men in the backyard garden. He had a natural instinct for this. He once captured all of the neighborhood kids. It was six against one, and Devin had all six of us tied to the apple tree in the backyard. He just left us there until we could figure out how to get ourselves free. We didn't, so a parent had to rescue us. That's the primary, and possibly solitary, comfort in all of this: Devin is doing what he was born to do. It isn't like I am the one over there, strapped to some gun I can't even hold and aim, much less shoot and hit. It is Devin. The young, little-plastic-gun-carrying, tin-pot-helmet-wearing boy, grown to full-grown, PT-record-setting, precision-shooting, award-winning Sergeant Devin King. Some days I let my fear and self-absorbency strip him of his skills, knowledge, and honor.

Some days my anxiety skyrockets, and my faith plummets, but Devin's talent and purpose always remain constant. It is the largest and smallest comfort all wrapped into one because, even though this is his purpose, I am reminded constantly that he isn't "playing guns" anymore. This war is real, and any casualties are permanent. He can't just pick up the little men and have another battle or hit the reset button on the Play Station. And I don't get a turn being the driver of the tank.

Siblings get overlooked in some of this. People seem more sympathetic when it is your husband, wife, son, or daughter. People have this, "Oh, it's just your brother" tone to their conversation sometimes. I guess if I were married or had children, I might understand that more. Or I guess if Devin were "just" my brother, I would understand it more. As it is, I don't quite get why anyone would ever feel that this is somehow easier for siblings, cousins, or aunts. Siblings are left in a unique position. We go through the process once for ourselves, and then again, each time we are in our parents' company. I have learned that you can catch all of the tears, but you can't keep them from falling. At least his absence has provided an opportunity to spend more time with my sister-in-law.

The amazing friendship I have with Devin has some downfalls. The major one is that he feels like he can tell me anything, which ordinarily wouldn't be so bad. However, when he tells me that he and his fiancée are going to go ahead and get married, and for what reason, then it's different. They were getting married so his fiancée would get life insurance, if worst came to worst. You just wish for that one second, and all the other millions of seconds those words are playing over in your head, that you were not on speaking terms.

Another disadvantage is that for my entire life, there has been this one person there to fight my battles for me. I depended on him way too much. This is the biggest thing to have happened to me so far in life. For the first time ever, he is not here to listen to me talk about my emotions and help me through this. For the first time ever, I am dealing with things alone. Devin is so special, so intelligent, and so strong that our entire family has had this way of making him the center of the universe. Part of the misery we're having while he's gone is that he's forcing us to grow up. Not a single one of us, from little sis to grandma, is ready for that.

Yet we receive letters and occasional phone calls from a man who is maturing more and more with each correspondence. At first, he was a torn young man who was used to living his life on his own terms.

But then, a commitment to country and a loyalty to loved ones brought about an internal struggle. Devin did not initially buy into his purpose and the US invasion on Iraq, but in a letter home he wrote:

> *I admit, I wasn't totally sold on our going to war with Iraq, and I was pretty frustrated when all of this started, but now that I am here and see all of this firsthand, I am so proud to be here. These people really need help. Hopefully when all of this is said and done, this will go down in history books for helping these people. I pray every day for them. They don't have anything. It makes me realize how fortunate I am.*

Those are pretty big-time words from the guy who left with his DVD player and Play Station in tow. It is one thing for the general public to question what we are fighting for, but when the soldiers themselves don't believe in it, it's a sad situation. Thank God it did not take Devin long to sort it out for himself. One of the many traits that has always impressed me about Devin is his intelligence. He has always been so wise and more experienced, known more, and had all the answers to my questions. I've always wished I knew as much as he does. Now he knows a secret I will never be able to comprehend. For the rest of our lives, you and I may not ever know why we really went to war with Iraq, but I hope to God that Devin never forgets.

When I think about the magnitude of what Devin is a part of, I only admire him and look up to him more. While it's the duty of every military person to serve their country, perhaps it is the duty of every person left behind to remind others what this side of military life is like. We are all directly affected by this, but some people are just too fortunate—check that, maybe they're too unfortunate—to realize it every single moment of every single day. That's just another one of the many frustrations: deciding whether to handle this like it is a blessing or a curse, knowing it is both, and wondering how to sort out the difference from day to day.

The war in Iraq is "officially" over, they say. Bull. Tell that to the wife whose birthday came and went. Tell that to the six-year-old who did not have Daddy at his soccer game. Tell that to my mind, when every morning I walk into the office and see headlines that read "Bloody Day in Baghdad," or "Suicide Bomber Kills 40," or "Another Convoy Ambushed." Devin and several thousand others are still over there, and we are losing soldiers every day. No one really understands what it is like to read those headlines and then skim the article for names. You hope you don't find out that way. You hope not to read it in the paper, but you know they would notify your sister-in-law first, and then your parents, none of whom would be emotionally stable enough to call you and tell you. With all of these embedded reporters, and the advances of the media, I know I could find out first from MSN.com. So I hold my breath and skim the paper, looking for names of soldiers or units, and saying to myself, "Please don't be 4th Infantry Division, please don't be…" Then it jumps out at me: "…the soldiers are from the 101st Airborne Division, names being withheld…"

Here is that moment where I want to swallow. Breathe a sigh of relief. I can't. Tears still come to my eyes, and my throat still burns because somewhere, there is a sister reading about her brother, or a mother reading about her child. Today is "That Day" for them. "That Day," when the war in Iraq is "officially" over. Yesterday, they still waited. Yesterday, they still hoped. Today, it is another process. I take a moment to feel for them, hurt for them. Then I take a moment to be thankful it wasn't Devin. Then I take a moment to feel guilty for that gratefulness. Then I go back: back to hoping, back to waiting. That is my cycle, minute after minute, hour after hour, day after day.

I love Devin. My heart is full of pride for him, but sometimes, like at 3 a.m. in the morning when I have had yet another bad dream, I am anything but proud he is over there. He may have been born a military person, but I have no such genetics. In my selfishness, I hate him. I hate him for missing Easter. I hate him for missing my birthday, his birthday, and his wife's birthday. I hate him for not e-mailing me a one-sentence e-mail every couple of days. I hate him for not being here when I argued with Mom last week. I hate him for not e-mailing me and saying, "Hey, wanna make a deal on helping me with a term paper this semester?" I'm "just" his sister, though. I imagine that whatever I feel, his wife feels ten times more, and I know that whatever we feel, Devin feels a million times more.

Mostly, though, I hate how life keeps going, and the world keeps turning. I hate how we already take for granted what Devin and the rest of the Armed Services sacrifice to protect. I hate the ones who say, "I saw this e-mail and it reminded me of you and your brother." I want to forget—until I get an e-mail, see an article, or hear a song. I can't. It's a constant in which moments pass, second by second, lifetime by lifetime.

My student worker told me that my pin with the yellow ribbon and Devin's picture on it was looking a little ragged. Really? My heart is a little ragged. My faith is ragged, and my patience is beyond ragged. She suggested I make a new one so it will be prettier. I guess she is like countless others who can see an American flag and NOT think of the soldiers still gone, or the others just getting ready to go. The flag is on so many t-shirts, so many hats, so many car antennae, that it has lost its meaning. We do not look at Old Glory and feel gratitude filling our heart, just as we are so saturated with crucifix jewelry that we no longer see Christ dying there. People do not look at Devin's pin and see the void in my everyday life. They do not see the hope or the fear or the waiting; it's just another symbol with its meaning forgotten.

I know that life as usual is vital. I do not want to begrudge anyone his happiness. I know that Devin and the others are over there for just that very reason: so we can all live in our little safe bubbles and gripe about such things as the slow drivers in the fast lane. I just wish we could all acknowledge and savor our happiness and our freedom. Mostly, though, I just don't want anyone to be fooled into believing the war is officially over. Nothing is over yet.

I know there are countless others who go through feelings similar to mine. As our soldiers battle overseas, we have become fighters here on the homefront. We struggle with the daily routines that once seemed so mundane. We learn all at once how weak and how strong we are. Even though there are several support groups, and even though people in your very own family are going through the same thing, you can't help but feel alone. Your pain is only yours. It is your hope, your fear, your faith, your loneliness, and your waiting. We use our weapons of faith, prayer, hope, and love. No matter how good the intentions of some, no one can quite grasp what it is like for you to have your soldier overseas. And how could they when even you haven't quite figured it out?

God bless America, God bless Sergeant Devin King, God bless each and every soldier, and God bless each and every family member. And God bless those who try to understand us.

"Their marriage philosophy is that no matter what it took, they would be in the same place together. So if one deployed, then the other deployed. They've put off having children for the sake of their marriage and future family, so they can serve their country together."

I'm Proud of My Baby Brother

By Kathy Reardon

Kathy Reardon's brother is with the 978 Military Police Company, based out of Fort Bliss, Texas, and deployed to Iraq in April 2003. Kathy Reardon lives with her husband, Ryan, and son, Grady, in Winslow, Maine. She is presently a stay-at-home mom and part-time graduate student, working towards her master's degree in rehabilitation counseling. Her younger brother, Sergeant Michael Cassidy, is currently serving in Iraq as a military police officer.

My "baby" brother is 27 years old. His name is Sergeant Michael Cassidy and he is with the 978 Military Police Company based out of Fort Bliss, Texas. There are four of us: Cindy, John, Kathy, and Mike—in that order. Our family has always been close, often referred to as "The Brady Bunch." So, when we received word that Mike would be leaving for Iraq in March or April, there was only one thing to do: fly from Maine to Texas immediately.

Our sister Cindy was already visiting Mike, his pregnant wife Maria, and their two-year-old son, Mike Jr., when I received a poignant call from her. Cindy explained to me that it was an experience like no other to be present among the preparations on base and to feel the heavy weight of wondering when Mike would receive "the call." We were crying and I said, "I feel like I need to see him." Cindy's response was, "Then you should come."

I had just quit my job a month before in order to be a stay-at-home mom, and the budget was tight. But when I looked at my husband and told him my feelings, he said, "Get the credit card. You should go." So I scrambled to find the cheapest ticket and left the next morning at 6:00 a.m. to see my brother. It was an overwhelming visit, lasting less than 72 hours round trip. It was also the most important thing I could have done and was full of more meaning and emotion than I can convey.

The most significant moment during the time I spent with my brother was the half-hour walk we took around his neighborhood.

It was 70 degrees, and Mike was in shorts. I was so cold that I was wearing one of his BDU jackets. The cold was most likely from the fear and anxiety that I felt for my baby brother. Regardless, I took a deep breath, pushed aside the tumultuous feelings I was having, and asked, "What are you feeling? What do you need?"

While that conversation will be forever etched in my mind, I will only share bits of what we shared. Mike's first words were that he wanted to make sure that he did the best he could to protect his soldiers. What followed, as his primary concern, was worry for his wife, son, and unborn daughter. He wanted to make sure that we, his sisters, brother, and parents, would support them in the way that he would not be able to do, being a soldier in a war. As is so typical of Mike, he was more worried about others than himself. He wanted to make sure that we all understood that he would have difficulty writing frequently to his wife, let alone the rest of us, and if we didn't hear from him not to get upset. To put it simply, Mike was intent on doing his best for his family, his friends, his soldiers, and his country.

It was at this point that I told him of the qualities that I have always admired in him. I told Mike that he is an honorable person. If you need a friend, there is no question that he is your friend. If you need to know that something will be done fairly and accurately, Mike is your man. If you need someone to trust, there is no one better then Mike. I told him that these qualities would get him through all of the challenges he would be facing.

The next morning, Mike, wearing his desert fatigues, took me to the airport. Two women approached him at separate times, saying, "Thank you!" "God bless you!" Riding the escalator to the terminals, I looked down and my last sight of Mike was of him, standing in uniform, with his hand raised to wave goodbye. We both had tears in our eyes. Never have I been prouder of my baby brother.

"It hurts so much, but it's a different pain. I feel abandoned, helpless, empty and sick."

Friends, Neighbors, and Strangers

Jenny McDonald Lovett

Josi Mata

Debra L. Winegarten

Leslie Forbes

Rachel Truair Farris

Mary Goodwin

Friends, Neighbors, and Strangers

The American Soldier - Time Magazine's "Person of the Year"

December 21, 2003. By Nancy Gibbs, Time Magazine.

"They swept across Iraq and conquered it in 21 days. They stand guard on streets pot-holed with skepticism and rancor. They caught Saddam Hussein. They are the face of America, its might and good will, in a region unused to democracy. The U.S. G.I. is TIME's Person of the Year"

The Little Red Car

By Debra L. Winegarten

The son of Debra Winegarten's friend is deployed to Iraq. Debra Winegarten is a native Texan. With a master's of sociology in qualitative research from The Ohio State University, she searches the past to bring alive stories of bold, brave people. Published in 2001, "Katherine Stinson: The Flying Schoolgirl," was a finalist in the Book of the Year award from Foreword Magazine and is now in its second edition and second printing.

Her lines were sleek; still, she harbored a station wagon body. And she was plump without seeming so, in an aerodynamic sort of way.

After the meeting, Michelle and I went to get in Kimber's shining new Saturn to be chauffeured home. Glancing over, I saw someone unlocking the VW's driver-side door.

"Hey Bee, great car!" I yelled.

"Thanks," she said in her delightful Danish accent, "I had one just like it in Denmark, and I loved it. This is Kevin's car. I love to drive it."

Bee got in and drove off.

That made me almost cry. Kevin. Isn't he the son in Iraq whom she hasn't heard from in weeks? The one for whom she fought with the optometrist assistant to get his expired contact lens prescription filled so he could actually wear sunglasses in the brutal 130-degree Iraqi summer?

I'll bet she smells him when she gets in his car, kind of like being surrounded by him. It's the closest she can get right now.

Mothers will do anything to stay connected to their children.

"Holy cow, Mike came home for leave and guess what... I'm pregnant! Holy cow!"

These Weren't Just Uniforms

By Jennifer McDonald Lovett

1st Lieutenant Jennifer McDonald Lovett, 51FW Public Affairs, Korea, has friends deployed to Iraq. She joined the U.S Air Force in 2001, where it was her job to facilitate media coverage for Operations Noble Eagle, Enduring Freedom and Iraqi Freedom, after the attack on the World Trade Centers. Her husband, 3-year-old daughter and she will be moving to Germany for her third assignment in the summer of 2004.

From the second floor of the wing headquarters building, a clear, sunny, Kansas sky was visible out the large windows of the lobby. Across the hall, the schedulers were planning routine training missions and watching CNN. Outside, the caretakers were grooming the hedges and trimming the green lawn. Downstairs, the commander, Colonel Ronald Ladnier, was holding a pre-flight briefing with local media who were scheduled for an orientation flight to refuel B-52s out of Minot, North Dakota.

It was a typical Tuesday for the 22nd Air Refueling Wing at McConnell Air Force Base located just south of Wichita, Kansas. I was laughing with Brad in the scheduling office, enjoying a daily ritual of jokes and banter that only good friends can share. Then CNN showed live video from New York of the World Trade Center tower that had been hit by an airplane. All work stopped as a muted shock rippled through the room. At that point it was fodder for gossip and speculation to break up the monotony of everyday work.

I walked back to my office and turned on the lobby television, asking my colleagues if they had seen it yet. Above Master Sergeant Scott Kerry's desk, the commentators were describing the situation and guessing at causes. Chatter increased in the office, everyone with an opinion. Being in the Air Force, we all had workable knowledge of aviation—enough to set off debate. Suddenly, another plane appeared on the small screen and in what seemed like slow motion, it slammed into the other tower. Now the air snapped with real shock and disbelief. I stared open-mouthed at the television. Looking around in panic, I searched the faces of my staff for answers. Their faces mirrored mine.

We were jerked back to reality when the ring of the crash phone blared through the office. I knew before I answered that what we saw on the television had caused that phone to ring—the phone that beckons the crisis action team to the command post. It washed over me. This was an attack.

Within hours of the crash phone ringing, pilots I knew were in the air shadowing the fighters guarding Air Force One. Within a week, two men with their security dogs from my husband's security forces unit were deployed to nations unknown, assigned to perimeter security. Over the next several months, I saw friend after friend deploy to Afghanistan and surrounding countries, or deploy inside the United States for Homeland Defense missions.

Then January came, and deployments escalated to an all-time high. I still wasn't called, but that was because I didn't have to go. The Air Force had picked two of my friends to go so I could stay home and work Homeland Defense.

John deployed to Cuba to support detainee processing, leaving behind his pregnant wife and two children for what was supposed to be a 45-day deployment. Carl deployed to an austere Middle East location for a 45-day stint to facilitate media coverage of the war. Both carried 9mm weapons, slept in tents, and had very little contact with family and friends. Their 45-day deployments lasted nearly eight months. The longer they were gone, the more I began to appreciate them and all the soldiers, sailors, airmen, and Marines I saw on the nightly news.

Back home, it was my job to acquire media coverage for our deploying troops, and tell their stories. And I began to attack that with vigor. This was my contribution to the war, however small; it was the only thing I could do to help. Meeting these people and hearing their stories gave me a profound respect for the people who choose to put their lives on the line for the freedom of others.

The first group we featured was one of 30 maintainers from the aircraft maintenance squadron, leaving to plus up the already 100 deployed airmen in the Middle East. It was their job to keep the aircraft maintained and serviced so the pilots could refuel the fighters and bombers. It was a domino effect to win the ultimate goal—bombs on target.

There was a crusty old master sergeant in this bunch who had been deployed before, and had been around for the first desert war. The calmest person in the room, he had a stalwart build that radiated overwhelming confidence. The younger guys looked up to him and knew they could count on his demeanor to keep things in perspective and get them through. Such a powerful thing to see.

Another feature we did was about two teams of services troops whose job it was to provide food, beds, linens, showers, and games for the service members. This team had a 19-year-old airman first class who had just graduated from basic training. She looked the reporters straight in the eye and said she had no fear because she knew her teammates were there to look out for her. What an incredibly moving thing to see, especially since processing remains was a core job for this group as well.

But the story that touched me the most was one of a married couple deploying together. Our security forces squadron was deploying 25 more of its troops, bringing its deployed total to nearly 80 percent of its squadron. Greg and Mary had met in a foxhole in Korea. Mary was pulling guard duty in a defensive fighting position, or foxhole, in the dead of a Korean winter. Greg was trudging through the snow banks along the perimeter, doing searches with his military working dog. He came to the foxhole; she asked if she could pet his dog, and they haven't been separated since. Their marriage philosophy is that no matter what it took, they would be in the same place together. So if one deployed, then the other deployed. They've put off having children for the sake of their marriage and future family, so they can serve their country together. Performing their jobs was the ultimate priority while they maintained the integrity of the unit. They packed together, fought together, and led their team of 25 troops together. And this year, that meant deployment to Iraq.

How strong their alliance is, and how dedicated they are to upholding the oaths they both made upon entering the Air Force.

These stories and so many more were important for the American people to know. These weren't just uniforms leaving behind family members to fly halfway around the world and fight in an unknown environment. These were human beings, each with a unique story.

The more I heard these stories, the more I wanted to do. Since they didn't need me in Iraq, I found the next best thing. The most forward-deployed air base in the armory sits 45 miles from the most heavily guarded border in the world—Korea. Hopefully, there I can do justice to the sacrifice of so many others. It wasn't futile, it wasn't for nothing. It was for everything.

"This is for you moms out there with sons and daughters in harms way far away from home. What would we do without your loving support and encouragement, knowing how difficult it must be? I pray for the safe return of all your children and wish they could be with you on your special day."

MISSING SOLDIERS' REMAINS RECOVERED

News Release Headquarters, United States Central Command, June 28, 2003

BAGHDAD, Iraq—Two soldiers, assigned to the 3rd Battalion, 18th Field Artillery Regiment, deployed here from Fort Sill, Okla., who were discovered missing on June 25, have been found dead west of Al Taji on June 28

—Courtesy by *News Release Headquarters United States Central Command*

It Is So Cold

By Rachel Truair Farris

Rachel Truair Farris had a brief, but touching, meeting with a soldier. Rachel is a 20-year-old equestrian professional in Austin, Texas. She loves her golden retriever, Gus. She says her connection to the war is broad but close to her heart, and wishes to acknowledge the sacrifices these soldiers make so that she can enjoy her freedom.

I was cold—the kind of cold that brushes against your skin and just chills you even more, as there was nothing left in my body that wasn't still absorbing the cold. The air conditioning was blasting in the Dallas-Fort Worth Airport on the 28th of June as I walked briskly toward the terminal to my connecting flight. I had been working for nine months straight, six days a week, with no holiday to speak of, in a frenzy of starting a new job at a just-born company. In my mind, my vacation to the Caribbean was well-earned, but as I strode hurriedly through the meat-locker halls of DFW, I still found my mind wandering to my job, worrying like I do best.

I was cold. Those were my first words to him. It is so cold.

I finally found my terminal... gate 23A, naturally at the farthest corner from my arrival gate. I remember checking my watch repeatedly. Seeing that the boarding call hadn't even been made, I gasped a sigh of relief as I turned the corner. Finally, I could pause and evaluate my surroundings, still quickly scanning for an appropriate place to sit.

I noticed him immediately. Not because he was in uniform, but because of the way he sat. His spit-polished boots were crossed at his ankles, the deep brown pants cuffed and pressed. His knees hung towards either side, not relaxed but relieved. Nothing about him was really relaxed. His fingers were threaded together, like one would do when praying, but his elbows rested on the arms of the chair, and his eyes were up, staring straight ahead. His shoulders were back, squared, and he stretched up tall in his chair. His round face had wide eyes that peered out from a protruding forehead.

He saw me. I saw him.

The terminal seemed empty other than him. For whatever reason, I took the chair directly across from him, smiling at him as I sat down, saying through my teeth, "It is so cold."

He smiled, nodding. "Yeah, that's the only good thing about traveling in uniform."

I inspected his lapels, attempting to gain some sort of information about him from sight. I noted a few medals and colored pins on his front left pocket, but knew from a quick mental comparison to people I'd seen in movies that he wasn't extremely decorated. A shiny engraved plate on his right pocket said MERRITT and I wondered if that was his last name.

"Are you in the…?" My ignorance of the Armed Forces was obvious—I knew his uniform was unorthodox. His hat was different, the color of the fabric a more muted brown with green undertones.

"I'm in the cav… the cavalry," He said with a shy smile.

"Really?" My knowledge of the cavalry was too outdated to discuss. Because of my interest in horses, I had done a research paper on "The Use of Horses in Wars Throughout History," where I wrote extensively about the cavalry of World War I. "How did you decide to be in the cavalry?"

"Well, I thought there would be horses in it." He paused. "I also wanted to wear the cool hat."

I laughed. I thought the hat was a little silly looking. "So, do you get to ride a horse ever?"

"No, I haven't."

"I work at a horse farm."

I guess I piqued his interest with that. Most people usually have one of two reactions—complete and total disinterest, or they want to know every detail of my job. I began giving him my usual speech—I had decided not to go to college so that I could pursue my dream of working with horses. He smiled gamely, and I couldn't help thinking how much his face defined the phrase "game face."

He looked up for anything, open to any idea or principle.

"So, how old are you?" This was the inevitable question for a person my age, working full-time, and traveling alone.

"Nineteen," I responded proudly.

"Really? Me, too."

Flying in a massive airplane filled with strangers is one of the most inherently bizarre and foreign feelings. Hurtling through the air at speeds of hundreds of miles per hour, you stare at the clouds you slowly pass through and can't help feeling the weight of everything you're leaving behind.

The day I walked through gate 23A at the Dallas-Fort Worth Airport to make the trek to my plane, I was cold. I had dug a warm sweatshirt out of my carry-on bag, but my skin still stung from the chill. All I could think about was the way Merritt sat, waiting for the next plane. Unhurried, enjoying the people that passed by, as if waiting were a gift. He was on leave for ten days from Iraq because of appendicitis that required surgery on the frontlines. In ten short days, the length of my much-anticipated vacation, he would leave his home in Iowa, leave his mother and father and whatever siblings he had, to return to Iraq, "somewhere north of Baghdad." After ten short days in his loving home, he would return to Iraq and "try not to get killed."

My heart ached for this young man, this boy my age, who stumbled upon his land mine destiny in the same way I stumbled upon mine—following our hearts, doing what we had been called to do in our lives. I never asked him if he wanted to fight, if his heartbeat shied from the sound of a gun, or if he ever closed his wide, round eyes, wishing he'd seen less.

The chill is still there. My only direct attachment to the war in Iraq is a baby-faced soldier from Iowa that I left waiting, fingers laced, ankles crossed, shoulders squared, in terminal 23A. A simple conversation I think about daily, a simple boy I pray for every night. I see his face, his eyes, his innocence and strength. I think of his parents; I think of all the parents. All of the sisters, brothers, aunts, uncles, and friends who have someone they know in the war.

A mere sixty words were exchanged between the soldier and me.

I cannot imagine sending away a lifetime of memories, someone I knew through and through, someone who had spoken a million words to me since the day of his birth.

It is so cold.

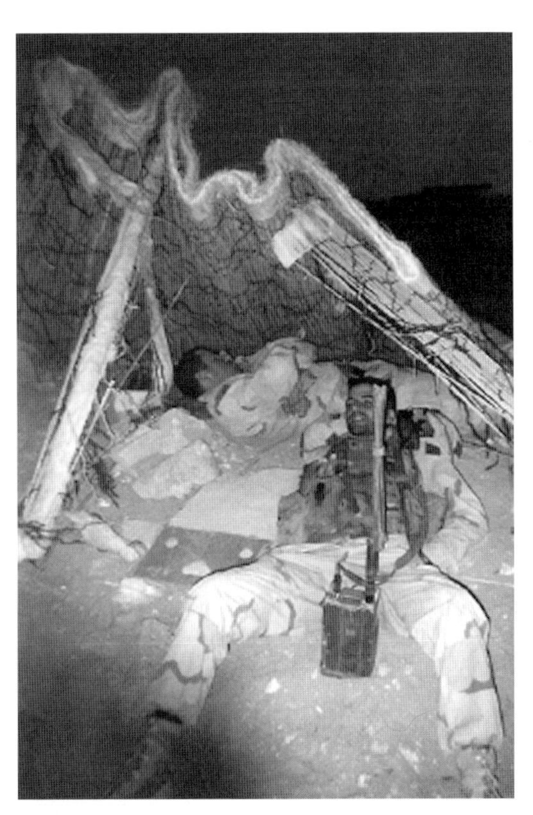

Soldiers resting at an outpost near the Syria border, Iraq, 2003.

"Once our service people come home, they tend to be forgotten. This must not happen."

"Thanks to all the great men and women who work their butts off every day to defend our great country."

River

By Leslie Forbes

Leslie Forbes is a writer, singer, artist and software engineer living in Round Rock, Texas, with two pit bulls, two cats and an untamed attitude.

I can imagine but I don't. In my strange way I believe it's disrespectful to imagine being in a war. So I don't—I simply try and listen to the news and piece things together. I notice things that I think are important and it leads me to piecing things together. I begin imagining and I think that's wrong. So I go back to square one.

I believe that normalcy is so tightly woven with insanity that if unraveled there would be nothing left of our society. The braid of the two holds us up in a living basket above the river Styx. Slowly each day we are lowered toward the black water. It's not the fault of sanity and it's not the fault of insanity. There is no fault to this machine. It simply lowers us one click at a time while the odor of oil reminds us what the muffling of metal smells like. It smells like machines.

Sometimes the basket swings in chaotic directions and the people go spilling out. Spilling out in Lebanon, in Sudan, in Palestine, in Iraq. We watch them drop over and down, down into the lumps of waves. Once they touch the water it's like they never belonged here in the first place. It's like they were visiting and have returned to their more natural, liquid environment. Their death surrounds every molecule of memory within us. Thoughts of them shoot off like arrows to the one ending bulls' eye.

To fall from the basket is separate and awful. To stay within the basket is considered natural. But we all end within the churning, lapping foam of death. War is not what makes us odd, it's that we have an idea that we don't belong in death and that others do; and we must lead them to their true calling. The camouflage of faith or the cover of ballots deceive us into actions which call up false hope in slowing our own journey into the river. Pushing some ahead of us we form a queue. Beings descend into murky waters ahead of us: No one realizes where they are in the queue. Everyone wants to know how to manipulate the line.

But what happens if you simply remember? You see the suffering and stare it full face in the chest. You do not move away yet your sensitivities will go wild and every hair on your body will feel singed. Sleep becomes your personal community theatre. The egotistical stars strut around upstaging anything once considered sensible. The defense calls you to the witness stand.

I can't imagine and I don't. I continue knitting, listening to the splash of bodies looking down to see the edge of a disembodied hand reaching up.

"Don't ask who of us suffered most during the deployment. Just remember we all suffered! Move forward, count your blessings and be thankful your soldier is home safe."

Maggie's Star

By Mary Goodwin

Mary Goodwin's neighbor's son is deployed to Iraq. Mary is a native of Wichita, Kansas. She and her husband have three grown children. She works on the staff of a large local church with a ministry team doing pastoral care. She has a Masters Degree in Christian Ministry and advanced Clinical Pastoral Education

The light in the front window of my neighbors' house first caught my attention last winter. It was always on. I was sure it had significance. It was a message to someone. Finally, I realized that the neighbor's military son must be serving in Iraq. Maggie, his mom, was keeping the light on as a beacon of love, so that Aaron could find his way home safely from a dark place.

It was true. Aaron was in Kuwait in the caravan moving north. For months, going and coming, I glanced up at the light as I passed.

A couple of weeks ago the window was dark. I'd heard the good news. Aaron was home on leave. His parents' driveway was full of cars. His family and friends were grateful for the reprieve from their constant anxiety, enjoying his presence in their midst.

On the night of his departure, I saw that the light in the window was burning again. The following day was deadly for the U.S military in Iraq. The local media came to interview Maggie. Of course, she spoke of what a fine young man Aaron is, and of his bravery—all true. Her eyes, however, were wide and yearning and spoke another truth. Maggie clearly wished things were different.

In the November issue of *Presbyterians Today,* Steve Yamaguchi writes, "Jesus teaches us to pray in a way that brings our long-distance vision into focus: 'Your kingdom come.' It is a prayer of hope and expectation. It is a prayer that keeps today's daily bread in perspective. It is a prayer that reminds us that the way things are is not the way things always will be." This advent season we are not waiting for the Kingdom in total darkness. Maggie's light is shining.

Adam Goes Away

By Josi Mata

Josi Mata lives in Pharr, Texas. She is studying archeology in order to bridge the gaps between traditional academic interpretations of indigenous peoples and the voices of the elders.

Untitled

With the sun came

the heartache

Everything is fresh and scary and too big

Such

A tremendous price to pay

My nephew in his Airforce uniform.. never been away from home

so proud

And hopeful Graduation

Boy, boy, littler boy, girl, boy, little girl, boy, boy

Crooked teeth, acne, wide eyes smile

everyone nervous hope

Fear, and a band, drowning out … everything .. why not everything

A horrible price for my boy

"Hi Mom! I'm fine. Miss you all! We are getting rid of the computers, so I'll not be able to write. We have also moved, but we're still here once every three days. I should be home at the end of March, but you will see me when I walk in the door."

Army Suicide Rates Increasing

Associated Press, January 15, 2004

WASHINGTON—U.S. soldiers in Iraq are killing themselves at a high rate despite the work of special teams sent to help troops deal with combat stress, the Pentagon's top doctor said Wednesday.

When This War is Over

By Peggie Knobles

Peggie Knobles, 80, is the mother of Lieutenant James Knobles, lost in Vietnam on September 11, 1970. Peggie is the daughter of a disabled World War I veteran, the wife of a disabled World War II veteran, and a mother who lost a son in Vietnam.

I have given a lot of thought about what to say concerning this war. The parents of the young people serving our country now are the age I was when my son was lost in Vietnam.

My dear friend, Dr. Victor Westphall, who also lost his son in Vietnam, spent his life helping parents and loved ones cope with their loss. He built a beautiful chapel at Angel Fire, New Mexico, to honor "All service people, those that did not come home, and those that came home broken in body and spirit."

When this war is over, Memorial Day will take on a new meaning for all of you. The Stars and Stripes will fill your eyes with tears. You will know what Francis Scott Key felt when he wrote, "And our flag was still there. . . ." Truly, "the land of the free and the home of the brave" is a freedom that is purchased with the lives of our brave service people.

Our disabled veterans will need our support. We will have to make sure the veterans' health care entitlement is met. Once our service people come home, they tend to be forgotten. This must not happen. I strongly urge you to help ensure that adequate health care services are available to all American veterans. Commander Billy E. Kirby once said, "The American people, indeed the free world, owe a tremendous debt of gratitude to those that have sacrificed their lives. Our country should always remember that many of our finest men and women demonstrated immense courage in making the ultimate sacrifice for their country." That statement is as true today as it was thirty years ago. I always end my letters with "Take care of one another," so to you I say, "Take care of our veterans!"

With much love,

Peggie Knobles

The Great Tragedy of War

It seems as if we might debate forever the reasons for, and the results of going to war, but there is one thing that we can never debate: the loss of life and deep wounds all around, and the extreme sorrow these families must perpetually endure. War brings sadness, despair and casualties on both sides, and a grieving heart does not have a nationality.

As of June 11, 2004, there have been 950 coalition deaths in the war in Iraq. There are 834 American casualties, 59 Britons, six Bulgarians, one Dane, one Dutch, one Estonian, 18 Italians, one Latvian, six Poles, one Salvadoran, three Slovaks, 11 Spaniards, 2 Thai, and 6 Ukrainians.

The US Army represents the majority of the casualties: 77.2%; the Marines, 19.7%; the Navy 1.9%; and the Air Force 1.2%. Casualties who were 24 years old or younger represent 46%. Women represent 2.6% of the casualties. I am aware that these are statistics, but very important statistics, because behind these numbers are real people—men and women with families and friends who love them. It has not been possible to find exact information confirming civilian casualties on either side.

When we talk about the ultimate sacrifice, we tend to think of all the men and women who lost their lives; but let us not forget those who returned home alive, yet broken in body and spirit. As of June 10, 2004, there have been at least 5,013 U.S. soldiers wounded in action.

Nobody knows what tomorrow will bring and how many more will have to suffer. Every day we live with the threat of terror and devastation in an uneasy coexistence with our hopes and dreams for a better future. I believe we can all do our part to make this world a better place for *all* of us. Just one small thing—one act of kindness, one vote, one prayer—might make a big difference.

I salute and honor all the fine men and women sent in harm's way. They fight unselfishly for you and me simply because they have been called upon to do so. I honor all the fine men and women who will not return home alive and those that have returned, broken in body and in spirit.

Bee Pedersen

June 12, 2004

All gave some, some gave all.

Statistical Source: U.S. Department of Defense

Iraq: A Country in the Middle East

Location: Middle East, bordering the Persian Gulf, between Iran and Kuwait

Area: *Total:* 437,072 sq km, *water:* 4,910 sq km. *land:* 432,162 sq km

Area—comparative: Slightly more than twice the size of Idaho

Land boundaries: *Total:* 3,650 km, *border countries:* Iran 1,458 km, Jordan 181 km, Kuwait 240 km, Saudi Arabia 814 km, Syria 605 km, Turkey 352 km

Coastline: 58 km

Climate: Mostly desert; mild to cool winters with dry, hot, cloudless summers; northern mountainous regions along Iranian and Turkish borders experience cold winters with occasionally heavy snows that melt in early spring, sometimes causing extensive flooding in central and southern Iraq

Terrain: mostly broad plains; reedy marshes along Iranian border in south with large flooded areas; mountains along borders with Iran and Turkey

Natural resources: petroleum, natural gas, phosphates, and sulfur

Population: 24,683,313 (July 2003 est.)

Age structure: *0-14 years:* 40.7% (male 5,103,669; female 4,946,443) *15-64 years: 56.3% (male 7,033,268; female 6,855,644) 65 years and over:* 3% (male 348,790; female 395,499) (2003 est.)

Ethnic groups: Arab 75%-80%, Kurdish 15%-20%, Turkoman, Assyrian or other 5%

Religions: Muslim 97% (Shi'a 60%-65%, Sunni 32%-37%), Christian/other 3%

Languages: Arabic, Kurdish (official in Kurdish regions), Assyrian, Armenian

Literacy: *definition:* age 15 and over can read and write *total population:* 40.4% *male:* 55.9% *female:* 24.4% (2003 est.)

Statistical Source: CIA – The World Factbook

Website Resources

Family support:

DeploymentLINK – http://deploymentlink.osd.mil/deploy/family/family_support.shtml

4MilitaryFamilies.com – an online support group, http://www.4militaryfamilies.com

Red Cross – http://www.redcross.org

National Military Family Association – http://www.nmfa.org/

Sgt. Moms - http://www.sgtmoms.com/home.asp

Army Morale, Welfare & Recreation – http://www.armymwr.com

Military Family Support Services - http://ww.bluestarfamilies.com/info_military_support_resources.htm

Deployed Military Family Support – http://www.dtra.mil/deployedsupport

PTSD support:

The Neighborhood Doctor – PTSD News, Research and Support Lists – http://www.yourneighborhooddoctor.com/list_ptsd.htm

Support 4 Hope – PTSD resource page,http://ww.support4hope.com/tds/post_traumatic_stress_disorder_understanding.htm

AEF – Aerospace Expeditionary Force. A term created by the Air Force Reserve to let reservists know when they might be most subject to activation or deployment. When an airman's unit is in its' AEF cycle, the airman knows he has a higher probability of being called to active duty.

BDU – Battle Dress Uniform, or fatigues.

CE – Civil Engineering, responsible for setting up electricity and power in a military compound.

Combat showers – Quickly taken showers where water is turned on and off only as needed to get wet and rinse off.

COMM – Communications Squadron, responsible for making sure phone lines are up and operational.

CONEX – Container Express, or a large metal container used to ship equipment over long distances.

E-4 – Enlisted rank, fourth up from the bottom. Enlisted rank goes up to E-9.

First Shirt – Nickname for the unit First Sergeant, generally the highest ranking non-commissioned officer whose main responsibility is troop welfare.

Flak jacket – Protective vest meant to deflect bullets or shrapnel.

Hummers – Nickname for the Humvee, the Army transportation vehicle that took the place of the Jeep.

ICU – Intensive Care Unit, where the most fragile medical cases are placed.

IMA – Individual Mobilization Augmentee. Within the Air Force Reserve, IMAs are traditional reservists who also fill a full-time civilian position and are subject to 'mobilization' or deployment in their military role.

In-process – The process of checking into a new unit or duty station.

j/k! – slang for "just kidding".

Kerlix – Sterile gauze used for bandaging wounds.

LAN – Local Area Network, or communications/computer network.

Leavenworth – A reference to the Army prison at Fort Leavenworth, where those convicted of crimes while in the Army serve their sentences.

Lima 5 – An additional skill identifier to a soldier's job position. In this case, the L5 identifier signifies that the solider has been trained in NBC reconnaissance, or nuclear, biological, chemical weapons reconnaissance. His job is primarily to detect the presence of NBC hazards and give first warning to his unit.

MIG – Russian or Soviet military aircraft.

MOS – Military Occupational Specialty, or job title.

NICU – Neonatal Intensive Care Unit, for premature babies

OUT PROCESS – The process whereby military personnel leave an area of duty or unit, up, to and including discharge from service.

Palletize – Put onto pallets for moving

PT – Physical training, or exercise.

PX/BX – Post Exchange/Base Exchange, the name given the stores found on military bases that sell both basics and luxury items to military personnel and their families.

R&R – Rest and Relaxation

Schmal winds – Fierce winds that blow on a seasonal basis in the Iraqi desert, kicking up sand so thick that it obscures vision.

Submunition - Any munition that, to perform its task, separates from a parent munition, i.e. bomblets.

Taps – Tune played on the bugle signifying the end of the day, or the death of a soldier.

Authors

Authors

News Bureaus and Organizations

Jim Garamone, American Forces Press Service - 5 & 25
Rudi Williams, American Forces Press Service - 11 & 44
Donna Miles, American Forces Press Service - 16
Mike Allen, Washington Post Staff Writer - 40
Jamie Reese, American Forces Press Service - 55
Steven R. Hurst, The Associated Press, Killeen Daily Hearld - 65
Gerry J. Gilmore, American Forces Press Service - 72 & 97
Maj. Gen. Odierno, From the Ironhorse Desert News - 87
The Associated Press - 92, 165 & 208
David Rohde with Michael Gordon, The New York Times - 105
Juan A. Lozano, The Associated Press - 108
Pfc. Sgt. L.A. Salinas, CENTCOM NEWS - 118
Kathleen T. Rhem, American Forces Press Service - 134
Robert W. Gee, American-Statesman Staff - 150
SFC Doug Sample, USA American Forces Press Service - 153
Chris Tomlinson, AP - 156
Michael Hedges, Houston Chronicle - 177
Charlie Brennan, Rocky Mountain News - 182
The American Soldier, Nancy Gibbs, Time Magazine - 193
News Release Headquarters, United States Central Command - 199
CIA – The World Factbook - 211

About The Author

Born in Copenhagen, Denmark, Bee Pedersen, former CEO, architect and world traveler, now spends most of her time weaving her observations and life experiences into short stories and novels. Bee Pedersen's first book, *A Dandelion is Also Beautiful* (translated from Danish) was published in Denmark and examines the life of a young boy dealing with the realities of a broken home and dysfunctional family. Her poetry has also been published in Denmark, along with many news and opinion pieces. Bee Pedersen's current writing projects span many genres, including suspense, women's issues and children's stories. Her book, *The Forty-Fitters* was published in 2003, and now she presents us with *Women Write the War.*

Bee Pedersen has always been interested in writing and languages. As a high school student, she studied Danish, English, German, Russian, Norwegian and Swedish. She says, "I have always written ... ever since I could put two words together. I have a wild imagination and strong desire to express myself. Writing is the perfect outlet."

Bee Pedersen received her Bachelor of Commerce in Internationalization from the Lyngby School of Economics and Business Administration and was awarded her master's degree in architecture from the Royal Danish Academy of Art. As an architect, Bee Pedersen renovated historical buildings in Copenhagen, consulted with the Danish Architect Group, and contributed to a humanitarian project in Tanzania. She then moved into management and IT consulting for several Danish and Norwegian companies, including DR and NRK Television, and the Danish Agricultural Business Association.

Bee Pedersen spent 15 years heading up global consulting teams for both U.S. and European software and consulting giants such as Oracle and Ramboll before starting her own software company. Bee Pedersen now lives in Austin, Texas with her husband, three sons and two dogs.